D1711554

THE KILLERS

THE KILLERS

A NARRATIVE

OF

REAL LIFE IN PHILADELPHIA

GEORGE LIPPARD

EDITED BY

MATT COHEN AND EDLIE L. WONG

PENN

UNIVERSITY OF PENNSYLVANIA PRESS

PHILADELPHIA

Published by
University of Pennsylvania Press
Philadelphia, Pennsylvania 19104-4112
www.upenn.edu/pennpress

Printed in the United States of America on acid-free paper
1 3 5 7 9 10 8 6 4 2

Library of Congress Cataloging-in-Publication Data

Lippard, George, 1822–1854.
The killers : a narrative of real life in Philadelphia / George Lippard ;
edited by Matt Cohen and Edlie L. Wong. — 1st ed.
p. cm.
Appendix 1: "Life and Adventures of Charles Anderson Chester."
Includes bibliographical references and index.
ISBN 978-0-8122-4624-7 (hardcover : alk. paper)
1. Riots—Pennsylvania—Philadelphia—Fiction. 2. Philadelphia (Pa.)—
History—19th century—Fiction. I. Cohen, Matt, 1970– II. Wong, Edlie L.
III. Life and adventures of Charles Anderson Chester. IV. Title.
PS2246.L8K55 2014
813'.3—dc23
2013047982

CONTENTS

INTRODUCTION

Equal parts crime novella and city mystery, *The Killers: A Narrative of Real Life in Philadelphia* showcases the wide-ranging political interests and formal innovations of its author, Philadelphia writer, labor activist, and reformer George Lippard. Over the course of a short but prolific career, Lippard (1822–54) published his own weekly paper, the *Quaker City*, and authored more than twenty novels, including his most famous, the wildly popular *The Quaker City; or, The Monks of Monk Hall* (1844–45), a lurid exposé of Philadelphia political corruption. "The critics never can accuse him of laziness—that is certain," remarked his earliest biographer in 1855.[1] *The Quaker City* was the best-selling U.S. novel before Harriet Beecher Stowe's *Uncle Tom's Cabin*, and it helped make Lippard a major literary figure. Little known today, in the 1840s, Lippard was read more widely than either Edgar Allan Poe (who happened to be a close acquaintance) or Nathaniel Hawthorne. *The Killers* offers a compact portrait of Lippard's narrative obsessions, his formal inventions, and his political commitments. It is spun around tales of gang violence, corrupt bankers, and inner-city racial tensions. It resonates today no less for its foreshadowings of the Occupy Wall Street movement, transnational gang warfare, and black market economies than for its valuable insights into key topics in American literary and cultural studies. It refracts histories of American race relations, the politics of immigration and labor conflict, the United

States as empire, transnational political and literary economies, and ephemeral popular literary forms like the city mystery and sensational pamphlet novel, directed toward a largely working-class readership.

Cheap popular print though it was in its day, only a few copies of *The Killers* are known to survive. After a brief description of Lippard's life and career, this introduction will offer cultural and historical background for reading *The Killers*, including a brief account of what is known about its publication history.

George Lippard

The fourth of six children, Lippard was born on a farm near Yellow Springs, Chester County, Pennsylvania, in 1822. When he was two years old, the family sold the farm and moved to German-town in northwest Philadelphia. Lippard had a hard childhood. Frequently ill, his parents eventually became physically incapable of working, and relatives raised him and his siblings. He lived with a grandfather and two maiden aunts who, facing increasingly straitened circumstances, were forced to sell off the family property piecemeal. Lippard moved to Philadelphia proper after the death of his mother in 1831. As a teenager, Lippard was intended for training in the ministry, but dropped out of a Methodist seminary at age fifteen. His father died soon thereafter and left his son with no legacy. Lippard, quickly falling out of good relations with the aunts who had charge of him, found himself more or less home-less in the middle of one of the worst economic collapses in the United States' history, in the wake of the Panic of 1837. Lippard found employment as an assistant in law offices, but the position paid little, and he quickly became disillusioned.

In 1840, Lippard turned to fiction, beginning his first long romance, *The Ladye Annabel; or, The Doom of the Poisoner*, which he would complete two years later. He got his start in the literary marketplace with a penny newspaper in Philadelphia, the *Spirit of the Times*, where he worked as a copy editor and city news reporter. During this time, Lippard presumably met Poe, who worked across the street in the offices of *Graham's Magazine* and with whom he forged a literary friendship.[2] Lippard began to make a name for himself with satirical columns; writing later for a paper called the *Citizen Soldier*, he wrote a literary-critical column called "The Spermaceti Papers" that furthered his fame. In 1847, as his popularity and success grew, Lippard married Rose Newman in an unconventional moonlit ceremony that took place overlooking the Wissahickon in Germantown. Family tragedy, however, continued to haunt Lippard, who later suffered the loss of his beloved wife and two children to tuberculosis. "Death has been busy with my home," mourns Lippard's prologue to *New York: Its Upper Ten and Lower Million* (1853), "death hath indeed laid my house desolate."[3]

Between 1842 and 1852, the literary historian David S. Reynolds estimates, Lippard published an average of a million words yearly in the form of sensational fiction, historical romances, public lectures, and critical essays. "In a day when Thoreau's social criticism went virtually unnoticed," Reynolds writes, "Lippard's took the nation by storm, provoking constant controversy and causing unprecedented sales of his fiction."[4] He hit his stride in 1844–45 with *The Quaker City; or, The Monks of Monk Hall*, which is thought to have sold sixty thousand copies within its first year in print. With the success of *The Quaker City*, Lippard became the leading figure of a new popular genre: the inexpensive serial sensation novel, which drew upon, while revolutionizing, the reporting of current events in U.S. cities. In the 1830s, the advent of modern printing technologies facilitated the establishment of penny press newspapers in all major U.S. cities, and sensational journalism, with its lurid accounts of crime, blackmail, and scandal, became a popular form of entertainment.[5] Lippard had begun *The Quaker City* as a seduction narrative, yet as its didacticism evolved, he "determined to write a book which should describe all the phases of a corrupt social system, as manifested in the city of Philadelphia" (2). In fictions like *The Quaker City* and *The Killers*, Lippard built a socialist critique of urban society through sensational depictions of city life that, while they used gothic elements popularized by the likes of Poe, prioritized arguments on behalf of the working class over aesthetic concerns. And while a writer for the masses, Lippard also distinguished his writing from the amoral sensationalism of the penny press, to which his writings were often compared.[6]

Lippard embraced an ardent democratic politics and protested the betrayal of the Founding Fathers' republican ideals in nightmarish visions of nineteenth-century America ruined by capitalist exploitation, religious hypocrisy, and class divisions.[7] In city mysteries like *The Killers*, Lippard exposed all manner of social inequities through highly charged "flights of the subversive imagination, and freely drawing on the irrational and grotesque" after the style of his much-admired predecessor, the Philadelphia novelist Charles Brockden Brown, to whom he dedicated *The Quaker City*.[8] At the same time, Lippard lashed out against the urban literary establishment, satirizing the vogue in feminized sentimental fiction while advocating a politicized national literature that aligned him with Nathaniel Hawthorne, Ralph Waldo Emerson, Herman Melville, and Walt Whitman.[9] Lippard's works pervaded the antebellum literary scene; from Whitman's early short fiction such as "Death in the School-Room (a Fact)" (1844), to the powerful but flawed reformer Hollingsworth in Hawthorne's *The Blithedale Romance* (1852), to Melville's depiction of city life in his novels *Redburn: His First Voyage* (1849) and *Pierre; or, The Ambiguities* (1852), the themes, stances, and stylistics of Lippard and his fellow city-mysteries storytellers can be found influencing U.S. writers across the canonical spectrum.[10] Indeed, Lippard's vigorous attacks on literary sentimentalism and the hypocritical paternalism of middle-class reformism that he associated it with would find their counterpart in postbellum America in the subversive humor of Mark Twain.

Lippard's moral stance was premised on a profound Christian faith, which, together with a resilient Jeffersonianism, underwrote much of his reform activity and writing. Lippard argued, for example, for land reform and free homesteading; against slavery, but with emancipation premised on land reform to prevent capitalistic devaluation of labor; and for labor unionization. Many of his other platforms—banking and prison reforms, for example—may be found articulated in *The Killers*. Lippard's founding of the Brotherhood of the Union, a national network of trade unions, is a good example of this vision. In his *Quaker City* story paper, Lippard began promoting the Brotherhood of the Union and serialized the tale that would become *The Killers*.[11] The popular if short-lived *Quaker City* realized Lippard's dream of founding his own newspaper and advancing social reform through popular literature unhindered by editorial intermeddling.[12] Based in local cooperatives, the Brotherhood of the Union envisioned labor unity across race, sex, religion, and trades. A national union, it nonetheless drew on both the rhetoric and the emotional disappointments (for socialists like Lippard) of the failed European revolutions of 1848.[13] The Brotherhood was a secret society, sustained by, in Reynolds's words, "a quasi-religious and patriotic ritual that would remind workers that they were members of a larger Brotherhood of Toil founded by Jesus and fought for by George Washington."[14] Four years from its founding, the Brotherhood could boast local circles in twenty-four states across the union. "The War of Labor—waged with pen or sword," Lippard once wrote, "is a Holy War!"[15] While tuberculosis would end that war for Lippard at the early age of thirty-one, the Brotherhood persisted; the same may increasingly be said for Lippard's writing.

The Killers

In one sense, *The Killers* is a classic tale of the Philadelphia in which Lippard grew up, a city viewed by residents and observers alike as a "laboratory for a social experiment with international consequences," in the words of literary critic Samuel Otter.[16] Here, the short story format favored by Poe forced Lippard to craft a more tightly plotted tale than he had in the digressive *The Quaker City*, resulting in a more unified narrative effect. Lippard's story begins in the (not so) hallowed halls of academic learning, at Yale College in the summer of 1846, at the onset of the Mexican-American War. But the plot quickly recenters in the landmarks of antebellum Philadelphia, taking the reader through the solitary cells of the controversial modern marvel of prison reform Eastern State Penitentiary, to the print shops made famous by Benjamin Franklin, and South Philadelphia's historic free African American community, whose denizens later provided the materials for W. E. B. Du Bois's pathbreaking sociological study *The Philadelphia Negro* (1899).

The Killers is a ninety-page sensational fiction based on the real-life events surrounding an infamous 1849 Philadelphia race riot. It is a tale of revenge, murder, gang violence, racial and ethnic conflict, international conspiracy, urban mystery, and, ultimately, working-class triumph. Fast-paced and wide-ranging, the story revolves around a corrupt Quaker-born Philadelphia merchant and banker, Jacob D. Z. Hicks, whose participation in the illicit international slave trade—banned in the United States as of 1808, but carried on by smugglers through the Civil War—begins a series of events culminating, in Lippard's fictionalization, in the California House Riot on election night, 1849. Hicks's abandoned biological son Elijah teams up with his disowned half-brother Cromwell to get revenge on their father, fueled by the money and secret rage of a Cuban émigré, Don Jorge Marin, whose father had been abandoned to his death by Hicks during a failed slave-trading voyage. This revenge plot intertwines with the story of Elijah's fictive kin sister, Kate Watson. Abandoned by his birth mother, Elijah has been raised as brother to Kate, the beautiful factory girl turned actress, whom Hicks attempts to abduct for nefarious purposes. In Lippard's fiction, wealthy villains like Hicks—representatives of the exploitative financial establishment—are also the monstrous seducers of female virtue, and by extension, the republican virtue of the young nation.[17] Like Hicks, Gustavus Lorrimer and Byrnewood Arlington, the immoral antagonists of *The Quaker City*, are Philadelphia merchants, and their seductions of two innocent women also drive that novel's convoluted revenge plot. In *The Killers*, Cromwell is killed by Black Andy, an African American grogshop owner hired by Hicks to kidnap Kate, while the gang that Cromwell leads, the Killers, burns down the bar. Don Jorge, meanwhile, attempts to steal Hicks's hidden money and is killed by a booby-trapped document box. Elijah witnesses the event and makes off with the money and a "merchant's Ledger," implicating "some four or five respectable houses in the profitable transactions of the African Slave Trade." Kate, saved from the burning bar by Black Andy before his own demise, joins Elijah; the two successfully blackmail the corrupt Philadelphia merchants and head to Central America to a new life.

The Killers is linked in instructive ways to contemporaneous U.S. literature, and it takes an important place in the international development of the literary gothic. Lippard drew on urban gothic conventions made popular in Europe and the Americas by French writer Eugène Sue's *The Mysteries of Paris* (1842–43), the most popular of the French *romans-feuilletons* (newspaper serial novels) and the rise of the "penny dreadful," the cheaply printed lurid British serial novels that began in the 1830s. Dubbed the American Sue, Lippard was often compared to the French writer who set his popular novel in the equally torturous back alleys and seedy groggeries of the Parisian underworld.[18] These European and American sensational traditions developed in reciprocal relation, although *The Killers* was published years before the English writer Wilkie Collins's *The Woman in White* (1859–60), which is often cited as commencing the British variant of the genre.[19] In *The Killers*, Lippard drew upon the tabloid-like stories of murder and intrigue featured in the recently established New York *National Police Gazette* and the lurid pamphlet publications that it helped popularize, such as *Life and Adventures of the Accomplished Forger and Swindler, Colonel Monroe Edwards* (1848), chronicling the exploits of an infamous confidence man who smuggled slaves into Brazil, Cuba, and Texas (thought to have inspired Herman Melville's 1857 *The Confidence-Man: His Masquerade*). The characterization of the sympathetic hero Elijah Watson, imprisoned for the crime of attempting to pass a counterfeit bill at one of Hicks's banks, also calls upon the compelling criminal types popularized by the British Newgate novel, which Lippard admired, particularly William Harrison Ainsworth's *Rookwood* (1834) and *Jack Sheppard* (1839).[20]

In this working-class hero, Lippard develops a powerful critique of the dehumanizing effects of solitary confinement in the experimental prison system pioneered by Philadelphia's famous Eastern State Penitentiary (also known as "Cherry Hill"). At the time, Eastern State, with its radial architectural design, was one of the largest, most expensive structures in the United States. It transformed Philadelphia into a world center for penal reform and a popular tourist destination on this account.[21] On his well-publicized tour of North America, British novelist Charles Dickens expressed a keen desire to visit "the falls of Niagara and your Penitentiary," the latter of which he later denounced in *American Notes* (1842).[22] Motivated by the rehabilitative value of incarceration, advocates of Eastern State's "separate system" (or the "Pennsylvania system") viewed solitary confinement as the pathway to penitence, for it prevented the influences of bad association endemic to over-crowded city prisons while allowing inmates solitude to meditate on the error of their ways. New York developed a rival program known as the "Auburn system," which housed prisoners in small, multitiered interior cells with communal workshops and mess halls. Unlike the costly Eastern State, the Auburn system achieved economic self-sufficiency through a rigorously enforced regimen of silent labor, typically lasting eleven hours a day.[23] Eastern State partisans, however, fiercely resisted reform and developments occurring elsewhere even as critics like Dickens and Lippard, who condemned solitary confinement as mental torture, began undermining public confidence in the system.

Watson's life after his release from Eastern State (where *The Quaker City*'s notorious evil character Devil-Bug once served as executioner) bears much in common with that of Clifford, the "wasted, gray, and melancholy figure" from Hawthorne's *The House of the Seven Gables* (1851). Like Elijah, Clifford suffers a long solitary penitentiary confinement that turns him into a "material ghost"—indeed, the embodiment of the "carceral gothic," in Caleb Smith's words—unable to readjust to domestic life once released.[24] "Solitary Confinement is a murder of Body and Soul," proclaims Lippard's *The Killers*, "It is the cruelty of the most barbarous age, sharpened and refined by the light and civilization of the nineteenth century." This critique of solitary confinement might also be read as a transatlantic rebuttal to Sue's argument for the humanizing reform of the prison system in *The Mysteries of Paris*, which charts, among other things, the vicissitudes of two orphaned Parisian girls, La Goualeuse and Rigolette, imprisoned for vagrancy. For Rigolette, imprisonment serves as a pathway to working-class bourgeoisification, for it transforms her into a resourceful and skilled seamstress.[25] The pleasuring-loving and improvident La Goualeuse also finds a blissful sanctuary in prison, only to fall victim to urban prostitution upon her release. Unlike Sue's romanticized grisettes (working women), Lippard's Elijah is an honest shoemaker pushed to criminal activities to survive. The events that follow his release—his failed effort to begin anew as a compositor at a print shop, his humiliating public dismissal as a former convict, and his desperate bid to join the Killers in a filibustering expedition to Cuba—offer a profound critique of the justice system and state authority couched in the melodramatic plot of filial estrangement and resistance against paternal authority. Lippard's preference for haunted and morally ambivalent protagonists such as Elijah Watson in *The Killers* also aligns his fiction with other outcast antiheroes from the American Renaissance, from Melville's Bartleby, Ishmael, and Queequeg to Hawthorne's Miles Coverdale and Arthur Dimmesdale. In this fashion, *The Killers* weaves together other important formal strains from antebellum U.S. literature: it draws on the reform tradition (albeit shorn of the middle-class respectability associated with it) of antislavery, antigallows, and temperance novels (such as Whitman's *Franklin Evans; or, The Inebriate* of 1842) and labor papers; anticipates Philadelphia-centric novels such as Frank J. Webb's 1857 *The Garies and Their Friends*; and may be regarded as a precursor to Martin R. Delany's *Blake; or, The Huts of America* (1859–62) in its depiction of the Cuban slave trade.

The exact composition history of the novella is not known.[26] The story first appeared as a serial, titled *The Killers*, over five weeks, starting at the beginning of December 1849. It was the last of five new serialized novellas published in the weekly paper *Quaker City*, of which Lippard was the editor. Very soon after, also anonymously, the pamphlet version, *Life and Adventures of Charles Anderson Chester*, appeared, with a fake publisher listed on the title page, almost certainly published at the expense of Lippard or his partner Joseph Severns. *Chester* was advertised as an "account," rather than a novella: "This work is no fiction, it is a true history from real life."[27] It seems likely that both the long and the short versions of the text were being prepared for publication at the same time, though they read very differently. *The Killers* was later reprinted with that title in book form (authored "by a member of the Philadelphia Bar," without copyright statement, and again claiming an apocryphal publisher), and as *The Bank Director's Son* with Lippard's name, in 1851 (see Figure 1).

Such a publishing path was not uncommon at the time for a sensational story based on current events. Printing the same tale in different formats and selling it at different prices reached a wider audience (and quickly), balanced investment, and was more likely to fulfill Lippard's desires of reaching working-class readers as well as wealthier audiences. *The Quaker City*, for example, had been published in parts, with some parts labeled as a "sequel," and then all parts combined to make a single title, sold first as a one-volume work and then in two volumes.[28] Keeping his name and an identifiable publisher off of the title pages of the various versions of *The Killers* until 1851 might have been a bid to make the story seem less biased, as Lippard by this point in his career was famous for his involvement in labor politics and other radical endeavors. But it might just have easily been a function of the fact

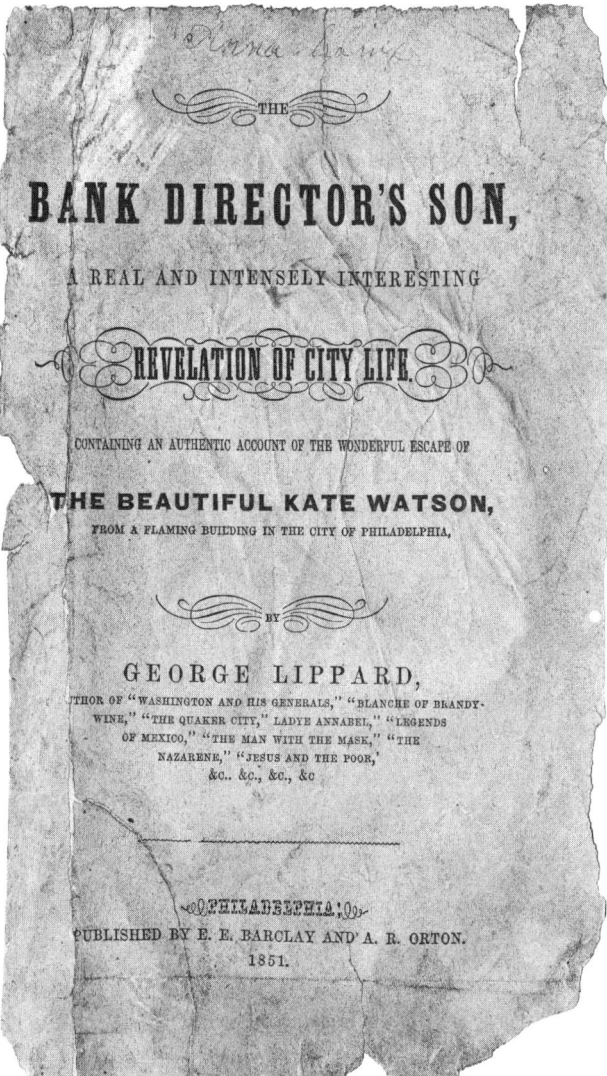

FIGURE 1. Title page.

George Lippard, *The Bank Director's Son*
(Philadelphia: E. E. Barclay and A. R. Orton, 1851). Am 1851 Lip.
Courtesy of the Historical Society of Pennsylvania.

that Lippard was more or less bankrupt in late 1849, and in debt to his partner, Severns, who controlled his literary output as a result. Or, as in the case of *The Quaker City*, anonymity might have been designed to avoid prosecution for salacious or slanderous content—or merely a way of attracting readers by implying that the tale was sufficiently scandal-worthy to require anonymity. The only known subsequent reprinting of the story happened in the 1960s, when a small press in Kentucky published *Charles Anderson Chester* as a children's story. Very few copies of the four original versions are known to exist.[29] Our edition is based on the book version of *The Killers*, which features few variants from both the serial version and *The Bank Director's Son*.

A new realism marked these later city mysteries that modified the excessive gothic irrationalism and salaciousness of Lippard's earlier works like *The Quaker City*.[30] An adulterous affair between a respected young merchant's wife, Dora Livingstone, and a foppish confidence man, Colonel Algernon Fitz-Cowles, drives *The Quaker City*'s revenge plot. Adultery recedes into the background of both *Charles Anderson Chester* and *The Killers*, which channel class conflicts through the parricidal impulses of vengeful scorned illegitimate sons. But the omissions, additions, and alterations of the pamphlet version of *Charles Anderson Chester* create a substantively different text from *The Killers*. Not only does *Charles Anderson Chester* leave out the Cuban subplot, the question of slavery, and the trenchant commentary on prison reform, but it also omits the complicated family dynamics key to the denouement of *The Killers*. Moreover, *Charles Anderson Chester* ends with the tragic death of Ophelia Thompson (recast as Kate Watson in *The Killers*), killed by chloroform in a botched kidnap, and she is named in a list of "the victims of the riot" appearing in the final chapter. In this, *Charles Anderson Chester* narrows the scope of its didactic outrage to the unchecked murderous violence of urban gangs while emphasizing the heroism of firemen like Charles Himmelwright, killed "while nobly engaged in the discharge of duty." In the variations between the two novellas, we see an author at work, experimenting with narrative structures, styles, and characterizations to hone an urban tale of class and race warfare with different political ramifications. While *Charles Anderson Chester* offers a pared-down narrative exposing Philadelphia's vicious underworld and the innocents like Ophelia whom it claimed as victims, *The Killers* offers a more complex tale of the international scale of capitalist exploitation, linking the contraband foreign slave trade to the domestic piracy of Quaker City bankers and merchants.

The California House Riot

The Killers also marks a shift in Lippard's working-class politics, as it charts the growing significance of racial discourse to Lippard's class protest (which would culminate in his last novel, *Eleanor; or, Slave Catching in the Quaker City*, serialized in 1854). On election night of 1849, the notorious Irish Catholic street gang known as the Killers (allied to the volunteer Moyamensing Hose Company and sometimes referred to as the Moyamensing Killers), provoked by rumors that the mulatto proprietor was living there with a white wife, attacked the California House, instigating a two-day riot. By taking what came to be called the California House Riot as the setting for the sensational climax of *The Killers*, Lippard—himself the son of Palatine immigrants who had fled religious persecution in Germany—responds to both the unprecedented influx of Irish and German immigrants into northeastern cities and the sectional politics of race and slavery in the months leading up to the controversial 1850 Compromise and its infamous Fugitive Slave Act.

At nine o'clock Tuesday evening after elections on October 9, 1849, a violent race riot broke out at the corner of Sixth and St. Mary (now Rodman) Streets. Such violence was far from unfamiliar in the site, which was roughly one block from where an angry white mob had attacked a parade celebrating West Indian Emancipation in 1842.[31] At the direction of William "Bull" McMullen, the charismatic leader of the Killers, the Moyamensing Hose Company rammed the four-story California House with a wagon full of blazing tar.[32] A desperate fight broke out between McMullen's gang and the African Americans residing in an area that was a mere stone's throw from Richard Allen's African Methodist Episcopal Church, the vital epicenter of Philadelphia's black population in the Seventh Ward. The densest concentration of African American households lived in the area between Cedar Street (officially changed to South Street in the 1850s) and Fitzwater Street and between Fifth and Ninth Streets. In 1848, a third of all the African Americans in Philadelphia resided in the southwest part of the Cedar neighborhood in Moyamensing Township.[33] Immigration in the 1840s and 1850s increased the Irish Catholic population in what became known as the Fourth Ward. By 1860, more than half of the foreign-born population lived in the outlying districts of Northern Liberties, Kensington, Southwark, and Moyamensing, which became part of the city proper in 1854.[34] Indeed, the loss of life and property in the 1849 California House Riot (following upon race riots in 1834, 1838, and 1842), according to Samuel Otter, galvanized the movement toward consolidating the original city and its new suburbs "with the goals of strengthening law enforcement and fire protection and extending the tax base to provide services for the expanded industrial urban center."[35]

But it was not just local civic leaders who found a warning in the violence. "Philadelphia," wrote antislavery activist Frederick Douglass in reference to the California House Riot, "has been . . . the scene of a series of most foul and cruel mobs, waged against the people of color—and it is now justly regarded as one of the most disorderly and insecure cities in the Union."[36] In its coverage of the "bloody riot in Philadelphia," the Washington, D.C., antislavery newspaper the *National Era* reported in graphic detail on the mayhem that ensued when "a gang of rowdies, styled the 'Killers,' furiously assailed the California House." After a desperate fight with black defenders, the Killers "broke into the house, destroyed everything before them, and set fire to the building, which was soon wrapped in flames."[37] Several of the adjoining houses caught fire. As the black residents fled the area, "the females," according to Douglass's *North Star*, "were pelted with stones by the rioters while carrying off articles of furniture."[38] The white rioters assaulted the rival volunteer fire companies that rushed to the scene, cut their hoses, and carried off the engines after shooting down a few of the members. Policemen attempting to restore order were also driven off. By the time the military arrived, the rioters had dispersed, secreting themselves away, but the area was left without any guards against renewed hostilities. At six o'clock the next morning, the rioters, now more heavily armed with pistols and guns, again mustered and renewed their attack upon the

African American neighborhood until the military was recalled and stationed in the lower district. "The companies," according to the *North Star*, "were assigned positions at the various avenues leading to the scene of riot, so as to command every approach completely."[39] Two men were shot dead the first night; a third died the following day; and twenty-five more were severely wounded with little chance of survival.[40] To effect greater verisimilitude, Lippard included a fictionalized list of the killed, wounded, and arrested in the final chapter of *Charles Anderson Chester* that was removed from *The Killers*. "There is not a city on the Union," admonished the *National Era*, "more shamefully mob-ridden than Philadelphia."[41]

The African American community in Philadelphia's lower districts responded forcefully to the attack upon the California House. In his 1873 postbellum slave narrative, James Williams recalls receiving a buckshot wound to his right thigh and "a blow over . . . [his] left eye—the mark of which is there until this day" in his efforts to help extinguish the fire that destroyed the California House.[42] In the characterization of the sole African American character in the novella, Black Andy, or the "Bulgine" (the name of a small locomotive used on the docks), Lippard offers a figural representation of this well-documented black resistance against the white rioters.

Initially enlisted in the fiendish plot to kidnap Kate Watson, Black Andy quickly loses interest in the scheme and "instinctively determines to save her" from harm, turning against his employer Jacob D. Z. Hicks, who has resurfaced in Philadelphia four years later after defaulting on creditors and falsifying his death. In the ensuing struggle, Black Andy kills Cromwell, the leader of the

Killers: "And over him, triumphant and chuckling stood the negro, *'Bulgine'*—the knife which he shook, dripping its red drops, upon his black and brawny arm." Two different illustrations of this chilling scene are found in the other variants of the novella (see Figure 2). Far more than a racist caricature, Black Andy, in full possession of his superior strength, taunts the drunken rioters: "Come to me, if you dar, you dam Killer tief!" Black figures often appear in

Prostrate on his face, the blood from the wound trickling over the boards of the floor, and over him triumphant and chuckling stood the Negro, " Bulgine," the knife which he shook dripping its red drops upon his black and brawny arm.

FIGURE 2. Black Andy, the late Cromwell Hicks, and Don Jorge.

George Lippard, *The Bank Director's Son*
(Philadelphia: E. E. Barclay and A. R. Orton, 1851). Am 1851 Lip.
Courtesy of the Historical Society of Pennsylvania.

Lippard's fiction; yet, these characters rarely drive plot development. Neither slave nor servant, Black Andy is the proprietor of the "Hotel," a grogshop catering to the multiracial denizens of South Philadelphia. Along with Black Sampson from Lippard's historical romance, *Washington and His Generals; or, Legends of the Revolution* (1847), Black Andy remains one of the more militant black heroes from Lippard's fiction, let alone in the city mysteries of other popular American writers, including Ned Buntline, George Thompson, and Augustine Duganne. He resembles the virtuous Richard Seaver, "a Chilian [*sic*] by birth," who became dubbed "King of the Negroes," from the serialized novels of Justin Jones (writing under the pseudonym of Harry Hazel), *Big Dick, the King of the Negroes; or, Virtue and Vice Contrasted* (1846) and *Fourpe Tap; or, The Middy of the Macedonian* (1847).[43] *The Killers* also prefigures the work of black Philadelphian Frank J. Webb, who would incorporate details from the 1834, 1842, and 1849 race riots into the plot of his novel *The Garies and Their Friends*.[44] It is important to note that such violence was not limited to antebellum Philadelphia. A few weeks after the California House Riot, the *North Star* reported another white-instigated "outrage upon the people of color" in neighboring New Jersey, where the "rowdies of Norristown emulating the 'Killers' of Moyamensing, attacked a three-story house in the east part of the borough, occupied by unoffending colored people."[45]

The duration of intense racial violence and periodic rioting characterizing antebellum Philadelphia—that "mobocratic city," in Douglass's words—was sustained in part by a volatile mix of factors that included, according to Otter, "technological change (the city led the industrial revolution in the United States), factory servitude, a rapid increase in the white laboring population, an economic depression that lasted with occasional recoveries from the late 1830s until the early 1850s, an expanding gap between rich and poor, inadequate housing, and political incompetence and corruption."[46] In addition, patterns of housing construction, particularly of cramped three-story alley homes, or "trinity" houses, built by speculators on cheap land located between large streets, allowed working-class African Americans and Irish immigrants to live in the same neighborhoods, yet not in the same community.[47] Lippard's climactic riot scene takes place in Black Andy's groggery located in "Dog Alley," a mere "one square" from St. Mary Street, "principally inhabited by negroes," where the actual California House had been located. This same alley houses innocent Kate Watson and her morally vitiated, laudanum-addicted mother.

Leaving the theater where she works, Kate takes a circuitous pathway home that leads her "[u]p one street and down another, now passing through narrow alleys, and now along the streets . . . until at last she reached a small frame house, which stood at the extremity of a dark court, in that district somewhat widely known as 'Moyamensing.'" Challenging the symmetry and discipline of the original city's rectilinear design (see Figure 11), Moyamensing's crowded, unruly urban labyrinth propels the complex, intersecting subplots of Lippard's *The Killers* just as *The Quaker City*'s gothic Monk-hall with its deadly maze of secret passages and trapdoors stands as an architectural embodiment of Philadelphia's Southwark.[48]

Runnel's Court, where Hicks uncovers the long-hidden truth of his paternal relation to Elijah Watson, epitomizes the cramped and squalid conditions of urban working-class life in these lower

"Either you must leave this house, or I will," said the girl, and dashing the gold pieces into the face of the portly gentleman, she retreated behind the table, her eye flashing and her bosom swelling with anger.

FIGURE 3. Kate Watson, her mother, and Jacob D. Z. Hicks.

George Lippard, *The Bank Director's Son*
(Philadelphia: E. E. Barclay and A. R. Orton, 1851). Am 1851 Lip.
Courtesy of the Historical Society of Pennsylvania.

"The devil's up in the City to-night, and men have been shot, who are worth your weight in gold,"—thus spake Cromwell.—
"One man wouldn't be missed much, particularly a man like you."

FIGURE 4. Jacob D. Z. Hicks, threatened by Bob Blazes
(a.k.a. Cromwell Hicks) and Don Jorge.

George Lippard, *The Bank Director's Son*
(Philadelphia: E. E. Barclay and A. R. Orton, 1851), frontispiece. Am 1851 Lip.
Courtesy of the Historical Society of Pennsylvania.

vice districts. Located in the liminal space partly within the "City Proper, and partly in Moyamensing," "Runnel's Court, in the neighborhood of Sixth and South streets," reads Lippard's pungent commentary,

> extended between two narrow streets, and was composed of six three story brick houses built upon an area of ground scarcely sufficient for the foundation of one comfortable dwelling. Each of these houses comprised three rooms and a cellar. The cellar and each of the rooms was the abode of a family. And thus, packed within that narrow space, twenty-four families managed to exist, or rather to die by a slow torture, within the six houses of Runnel's Court. Whites and blacks, old and young, rum-sellers and their customers, were packed together there, amid noxious smells, rags and filth, as thick and foul as insects in a decaying carcase.

Traversing between the old city and its newer outlying districts, *The Killers*' depiction of the geography, politics, and history of Philadelphia's race riots helped constitute Lippard's unique "aesthetics of place," in Otter's words.[49]

Philadelphia native and Reconstruction-era politician Mifflin Wistar Gibbs vividly recalled the "ravages of what was known as the 'Moyamensing Killers,' who burned down the churches and residences of the colored people and murdered their occupants."[50] In his memoir, *Shadow and Light: An Autobiography* (1902), Gibbs remarked upon the forces, both social and economic, that propelled Irish racial differentiation: "The Irish, having fled from oppression in the land of their birth, for notoriety, gain, or elevation by comparison, were nearly all pro-slavery."[51] Labor competition in antebellum Philadelphia intensified the need to reestablish racial distinctions between white and nonwhite. The California House Riot pitted working-class Irish labor immigrants against working-class black labor migrants and undermined the idealized vision of class-based solidarity that Lippard sought to disseminate in his political writings.[52] In *The Quaker City*, the minor character of Pump-Handle, a member of Devil-Bug's vagabond crew anticipates the riotous denouement of *The Killers* in his recitation of crimes for which he had been convicted: "'Why you see, a party of us one Sunday arternoon, had nothin' to do, so we got up a nigger riot. We have them things in Phil'delphy, once or twice a year, you know? I helped to burn a nigger church, two orphans' asylums and a school-house. And happenin' to have a pump-handle in my hand, I aksedentally hit an old nigger on the head. Konsekance wos he died'" (482). Pump-Handle's nonchalant recitation of brutality and murder illuminates the numbing regularity of working-class racial violence in antebellum Philadelphia.

In the months before the riot, Lippard published in his weekly story paper the *Quaker City* an outraged response to a critic who had reviled him as "fanatical" on the subject of "Black Slavery," writing, "Can we attack Wage Slavery and be silent about Chattel Slavery? Are we to hold our peace about the enslavement of white men, because the discussion of that topic involves a review of the nature and results of Black Slavery?"[53] Such cross-racial identifications, according to Timothy Helwig, were not unique in Lippard's writings, particularly in his city mysteries, which often paired class consciousness with antislavery discourse.[54] In an effort to resolve the contradictions of "free labor," Lippard radically reenvisions the historic conditions of the California House Riot in *The Killers*. He minimizes the ethnic divisions fracturing white working-class solidarity by eliding the Irish Catholic presence from the race riot, although he fashions for the young villain Cromwell a comical Irish "confidential servant" named Patrick who speaks in the "richest Hibernian." In Lippard's fictionalization, Cromwell initiates the riot, directing the Killers to "raise the devil among the niggers of Mary street" as a cover for an elaborate revenge plot against his father. Cromwell, the slave trader turned filibustering adventurer, exploits the Moyamensing men for his own purposes just as his corrupt banker father Hicks takes advantage of the election night bedlam to kidnap Kate. Hicks's kidnapping plot alludes to the scandalous 1843 murder case involving a prominent Philadelphian, Singleton Mercer, who had revenged himself upon a young gallant named Mahlon Heberton for the kidnap and seduction of his sister. Lippard partly based *The Quaker City* on Mercer's murder trial, and he returned to this plot device in *The Killers*.[55] The final lines of the novella draw a critical analogy between father and son, linking the Philadelphia race riot, the international slave trade, and the Cuban annexation campaign as interrelated symptoms of a larger class and race crisis in its portrayal of the "Merchant and his confederates" as "Respectable Killers." Lippard's introduction to the version of the novella first serialized in the newspaper the *Quaker City* had made even more explicit this comparison: "The Killer of Moyamensing, drunk on bad brandy, and filthy with the mud of the kennel—reeking at once with rum and blood—is a decent, honest, and respectable man, compared to his smooth Brother—the Killer who skulks behind the Charter of a Bank" (see Appendix 2).[56]

Significantly, it is Black Andy (and not the sympathetic white working-class hero Elijah Watson) who single-handedly thwarts both diabolical plots. His heroic effort to save the innocent Kate re-signifies the rumored interracial relationship that instigated the actual attack upon the California House and allows Lippard to imagine a transient instance of solidarity across the divisions of class and race. Atop the burning grogshop, the powerful silhouette of Black Andy holding aloft the insensible Kate momentarily arrests the chaotic cacophony of the riot. In this brief, melodramatic moment, all those involved in the riot, from "negroes and whites, firemen and Killers" to "spectators at distant windows," cry out in unison, joined together in the common purpose to "Save the gal!" This dramatic effort to rescue virtuous womanhood reveals the possibilities of black and white coexistence and working-class coalition joined in a noble, albeit masculinized, cause.

In *The Quaker City*, Lippard associated blackness with the denizens of Philadelphia's underworld, particularly in the racially ambiguous figure of Devil-Bug, the murderous keeper of the house of vice. While Monk-hall's grand rooms host "the eloquent, the learned, and . . . the pious of the Quaker City" in riotous scenes of corruption and debauchery, its cavernous underground recesses house the "Outcasts of the Quaker City," a vagabond "mass of rags and lameness, filth and crime" over whom Devil-Bug rules as patriarch aided by two hulking black henchmen named Glow-worm and Musquito (476, 477). By describing Glow-worm and Musquito as "dressed in . . . flaring red flannel shirt[s]," Lippard links his black characters to the working-class consciousness embodied in local fire companies and their associated street gangs who were identified by their distinctive red flannel shirts (52).[57]

In fact, Lippard had initially envisioned the connection between blackness and working-class consciousness in the character of Devil-Bug, whom he described in a playbill for the censored theatrical adaptation of the novel (recently recovered by Sari Altschuler and Aaron Tobiason) as "a Negro, deeply dyed in crime."[58] Critics often cite Devil-Bug's apocalyptic vision of the future as a powerful instance of Lippard's critical linkage of wage with chattel slavery: "Then came the slaves of the city, white and black, marching along one mass of rags and sores and misery, huddled together . . . the slaves of the cotton Lord, and the factory Prince" (389). Lippard further develops this cross-racial economic critique in the character of Black Andy whose heroic effort to save Kate revises the more brutish "Black Herkles" of *Charles Anderson Chester.* Kate's rescue redeems Black Andy's questionable moral virtue, while his murder of Cromwell, the leader of the Killers, takes on vigilante significance as the city reels from the ruinous destruction of the race riot that his gang has instigated.

The Philadelphia Underworld and the Moyamensing Killers

By the 1840s, the Moyamensing street gang known as the Killers had become the largest of more than fifty gangs prowling Philadelphia at the time, which included the Whelps, Bouncers, Flayers, Shifflers, Hyenas, Schuylkill Rangers, Buffers, Forty Thieves, Snakers, Stingers, Smashers, Gumballs, Rats, and Bloodtubs.[59]

With their growing notoriety, the Killers also became the subject of cheap sensational fiction, such as *The Almighty Dollar;*

TWO OF THE KILLERS.

Figure 5. "Two of the Killers."

Lithograph. Philadelphia: John Childs, 1848. Print Dept. W408 [P.2219].
Courtesy of the Library Company of Philadelphia.

or, The Brilliant Exploits of a Killer: A Thrilling Romance of Quakerdelphia (1847), which fashioned the Killers as proletarian heroes fighting "the scourge of vassalage . . . the iron-sway of the rich" even though its members were "mostly under twenty, of the ragamuffin and utterly depraved order, and undoubtedly the hardest cases to be found within the precincts of Quakerdelphia county."[60] "[O]ur strength," exclaim the gathered Killers in *The Almighty Dollar*, "lies in the district of Moyamensing, and Moyamensing must be our stronghold" (15). In the ensuing arson trial of Robert, the leader of the Killers, the judge addresses the jury, declaring in no uncertain terms, "no one is safe at night in Moyamensing, wayfarers are plundered and injured, the inhabitants have to suffer insults and losses, no one dares INFORM, for then his all would be sacked and burnt; ALL LAW is set at defiance, the grossest species of inequity prevail, the DISTRICT had become a nest for villains of every CALIBRE and DYE; SUCH ARE THE KILLERS AND THE AWFUL EFFECTS OF THEIR CLUB" (34). In similar fashion, Lippard's title page represents his novella as a thrilling exposé of the Killers' reign of terror in Philadelphia's lower districts: "In which the deeds of the Killers, and the great Riot of election night, October 10, 1849, are minutely described."[61] The nefarious exploits of urban gangs like the Moyamensing Killers became a mainstay of the salacious, muckraking city-mysteries genre, popularized in the sensational fictions of another writer, Ned Buntline, a contemporary of Lippard's, whose *The B'hoys of New York* (1850), a sequel to his successful *Mysteries and Miseries of New York* (1848), also features a Cuban filibustering subplot.

The Moyamensing Hose Company was one of the many volunteer companies that serviced Philadelphia.[62] Often allied with local gangs, these hose companies and their violent rivalries became the subject of growing concern in the city, and didactic reform novellas such as H. C. Watson's *Jerry Pratt's Progress; or, Adventures in the Hose House, Based on Facts* (1855) illustrated the moral ills associated with the "Hose and Engine Houses . . . notorious as the haunts of the idle and depraved—as nurseries of vice—as the scenes of the ruin of many youths of promise."[63]

In his 1893 memoir, journalist and folklorist Charles Godfrey Leland (1824–1903), a Philadelphia native, offered a scathing account of these companies and the reign of terror over the city that lasted until their elimination in 1871:

FIGURE 6. Hope Hose Company.

Photograph. Philadelphia: James E. M'Clees, 1858. Photo—McClees [(6)1322.F.120].
Courtesy of the Library Company of Philadelphia.

Whoever shall write a history of Philadelphia from the Thirties to the end of the Fifties will record a popular period of turbulence and outrages so extensive as to now appear almost incredible. These were so great as to cause grave doubts in my mind whether the severest despotism, guided by justice, would not have been preferable to such republican license as then prevailed in the city of Penn. I refer to the absolute and uncontrolled rule of the Volunteer Fire Department, which was divided into companies (each having clumsy old fire apparatus and hose), all of them at deadly feud among themselves, and fighting freely with pistols, knives, iron spanners, and slung shot. Of these regular firemen, *fifty thousand* were enrolled, and to these might have been added almost as many more, who were known as runners, bummers, and hangers-on. Among the latter were a great number of incendiaries, all of whom were well known to and encouraged by the firemen. Whenever the latter wished to meet some rival company, either to test their mutual skill or engage in fight, a fire was sure to occur; the same always happened when a fire company from some other city visited Philadelphia.[64]

Leland recalled "hearing ladies who lived in Pine Street describe how, on Sunday summer afternoons, they could always hear . . . the shots of the revolvers and shouts of firemen as they fought in Moyamensing" (218). The "southern part of the city was a favorite battleground" for these rival companies, and William McMullen, the undisputed leader of the Killers and the Moyamensing Hose Company to which the gang was allied, ruled this lower district.

The son of an Irish immigrant, "Squire McMullen" would become the stuff of local legend: the subject of multiple failed assassination attempts by rival Shiffler Hose Company (named after George Shiffler, purported to have been killed by McMullen during a nativist riot involving Catholics and Protestants that engulfed Kensington in 1844 and served as the backdrop for Lippard's unfinished 1846 serialized city-mysteries novel *The Nazarene; or, The Last of the Washingtons*, the sequel to *The Quaker City*). McMullen would become, according to his 1901 obituary in the Philadelphia *Public Ledger*, "one of the best known men in local politics."[65] The proprietor of a popular tavern (at Eighth and Bainbridge Streets) catering to the Killers and Moyamensing Hose Company, McMullen later became a ward leader.[66] His varied exploits drove his political career, leading to his appointment to the board of inspectors for Moyamensing Prison and election as alderman in 1857.[67] A Jacksonian Democrat, the young McMullen had evaded trial and likely imprisonment for attacking two Southwark policemen by enlisting for a tour of duty in the Mexican-American War (1846–48). McMullen and the Moyamensing men, many of whom were also Killers, became part of Company D of the First Pennsylvania Infantry assigned to General Robert Patterson's brigade.[68] McMullen quickly assumed leadership of the company. Kirsten Silva Gruesz writes that the "twenty-months' war that followed, involving a full-scale invasion of central Mexico by land, a siege of the capital and its principal port, and a military expedition across the far western portion of the continent to Santa Fe, radically changed the balance of power in the Americas, arguably turning the United States into an imperial power."[69] McMullen and his men returned to Philadelphia as heroes.[70]

The young McMullen may have inspired Lippard's portrayal of Cromwell Hicks in his reincarnation as "Bob Blazes, the Captain of the Killers," once he puts aside his disguise as "the Loafer," in a plot device drawn from *The Quaker City*'s antihero Luke Harvey, who also masks himself as "Brick-Top, a Loafer" to trap Devil-Bug. It is not a coincidence that Lippard pointedly alludes to Cromwell's elaborate scheme to attack the California House as "his plan of operations for the Mexican Campaign." Initially, Lippard had lent enthusiastic support to the Mexican-American War, but he later changed his views.[71] In the second half of the novella, Lippard reintroduces Cromwell as the leader of a band of Killers hand-selected for a filibustering expedition to Cuba. "In a week, my boys, we'll start for Cuba," Blazes greets his "brawny fellows," "'Cuba, gold, and Spanish women,' that's our motto! You know that I'm in communication with some of the heads of the Expedition; I was told to pick out the most desperate devils I could find in Moyamensin'. I've done so. You've signed your names, and received your first month's pay. In a week you'll go on to New York with me, and then hurrah for 'Cuba, gold, and Spanish women!'"

The dynamics of U.S. empire building had driven the Mexican-American War, which ended in a territorial purchase forced upon a weakened, divided, and impoverished nation, according to Gruesz.[72] After the Mexican-American War, Hispano-Anglo alliances set their sights on the annexation of Cuba, which had been the object of U.S. purchase offers for three decades.[73] "Cuba, by geographical position, necessity and right, belongs to the United States; it may and must be ours," proclaimed an editorial in 1847.[74] Playing upon "the national lust of territorial aggrandizement and universal empire," U.S. expansionists touted Cuba's strategic naval and commercial location to American Manifest Destiny: "Its possession would give us command of the Archipelago and all the neighboring seas, so that on island and continent, land and water, our power would be supreme."[75]

Cuban Annexation and the Foreign Slave Trade

Lippard may have drawn from pro-slavery Narciso López's highly publicized recruitment campaigns for a filibustering expedition to Cuba (eventually blocked by President Zachary Taylor in 1850) in crafting the Cuban subplot of *The Killers* (and referenced in *Charles Anderson Chester* as "the celebrated Cubian [*sic*] expedition").[76] In the month before the California House Riot, newspapers reported on the "unusual number of Cubans . . . visiting New York." Like the character of Don Jorge, these "transient Cubans" were "young men, attached to wealthy and respectable families, of good education, but ardent, undisciplined, hot-blooded . . . ripe for rebellion and revolution."[77] Another issue of the same paper speculated that the "secret expedition against Cuba" might have been "under the supervision of the refugees from Cuba . . . acting in concert with conspirators here."[78] Early national Philadelphia— "la famosa Filadelfia," as it was called—emerged as a center for Hispanophone print culture during the years that Lippard was growing up there. Of all the northeastern cities, it figured most centrally in the independence movements against Spanish colonial rule throughout Latin America and the Caribbean.[79] Lippard alludes to this Hispanophone history in Don Jorge's portrayal of his father (who appears variously as Captain Velasquez and Antonio

Marin, also the name of a Mexican officer in Lippard's 1848 *'Bel of Prairie Eden: A Romance of Mexico*) as a political refugee, "a native of Cuba, who for political offences had been exiled" and who passes his days "engaged upon some attempt or other to free [his] native Island from the Spaniard."

Such rumors and intimations of a Hispano-Anglo plot to annex slaveholding Cuba threatened ongoing antislavery efforts on U.S. soil, for Cuban annexation as a potential slave territory (as in the recently acquired Texas) would give "the Slave Power the preponderance in our National Legislature, and strengthen and confirm the hateful system in the States where it now exists."[80] Indeed, abolitionists sought to demonstrate "how the necessities of slavery have mixed up our affairs with foreign interests, and infused into our diplomacy base principles and a spirit of dark intrigues."[81] Foremost among these anti-annexation abolitionists stood Martin R. Delany, one of the earliest proponents of black nationalism, who, in April 1849, warned *North Star* readers of "a deep-concerted scheme for the annexation of Cuba to the United States." Cuba, as Delany cautions, "is the great channel through which slaves are imported annually into the United States, contrary to the law of the land, and the sovereign power by which the constitutional power of 1808 is stricken down, and made null and void at the will of the slaveholder."[82] Delany describes the circuitous route by which men like the notorious Monroe Edwards and Lippard's fictional Don Jorge and Cromwell circumvent the 1808 ban against the importation of foreign slaves into the United States:

> Into this island are there annually imported more than
> fifty thousand slaves, expressly for the human market,

and being contiguous to the United States, vessels from Baltimore, Washington city, Richmond, and other American slave-markets usually after shipping a *few* slaves purchased in those particular places, sail to the isle of Cuba under the pretext of touching by Havana for trade. When they enter the barracoons, the traders to whom the slaves on board belong, frequently the master and owner of the vessel being concerned in the traffic, purchase a full cargo of slaves, sail to New Orleans where they are sold out to the highest bidder, at the slave market there, from whence they are taken to all parts of the South. In this high-handed manner is the provision prohibiting the importation of slaves into the United States after the year 1808, openly and constantly trampled under foot; and those in power, the supreme Judicial and Executive authorities being generally slaveholders or their abettors, well know these facts, and by keeping silence wink at and encourage such undisguised, infamous deeds of daring.[83]

As in Lippard's *The Killers*, the intertwined subplots of Cuban annexation and the illegal foreign slave trade would drive the second part of Delany's famously unfinished serialized novel, *Blake; or, The Huts of America.*

In Lippard's novella, Don Jorge entices a circumspect Cromwell with the seemingly benign vision of Cuba as "an island in the gulf . . . with many a snug cove to shelter a craft which has not been properly cleared at the Custom House." After four years in the foreign slave trade, Cromwell returns to Philadelphia battle-scarred and ferocious. He seizes leadership of the Killers, entertaining the ruffian lot with his tales of "life in Havana—of life on the coast of Africa—of slave ships stored thick and foul with their miserable cargo—and of the manner in which certain mercantile houses, in the north, made hoards of money, even at the present day, by means of the Slave Trade." *The Killers* concludes with a footnote citing an extract from President Taylor protesting "that barbarous traffic," which continued illicitly in the United States despite congressional efforts in 1820 to enforce the 1808 abolition by declaring participation in the foreign slave trade to be an act of piracy punishable by death. At the end, the novella comes full circle, given the coded references to "piracy" that punctuate Don Jorge's initial efforts to lure the young Cromwell into participating in his slave-trading scheme. By identifying Cuban annexation with the foreign slave trade, Lippard refuses to resolve his violent, tangled gothic plot of urban class and racial formations in an appeal to U.S. expansionism, revising the empire-building stance he promoted in his two earlier Mexican-American War novels, *Legends of Mexico* (1847) and *'Bel of Prairie Eden* (1848).[84]

The complex, intersecting plotlines of Lippard's *The Killers* gradually enfold the race, class, and immigration conflicts erupting in urban Philadelphia within the framework of the transatlantic slave trade and U.S. economic ties to the global South. Cromwell Hicks and Don Jorge, agents of conspiracy and race riot, not only have ties to fathers implicated in the foreign slave trade, but they seek to reengage the United States in that international traffic.[85] According to "popular rumor," Hicks is descended from an old Quaker family whose wealth "had been acquired in the slave trade at a time when the slave trade was as legal, moral, and religious, as stock gambling at the present day." In addition to this primitive accumulation, Hicks further augments the family fortune by engaging in the now-illegal foreign slave trade with Velasquez, whom Hicks later betrays and leaves to "rot in jail, on the charge of piracy" after their vessel is "seized off the Brazil coast." *The Killers* thus reveals the *longue durée* of class formations in northeastern cities as inseparable from the slave trade and U.S. imperial expansion—what Shelley Streeby describes as the "nexus of city and empire" characterizing Lippard's writings.[86] Moreover, Lippard casts a disparaging eye upon the liberation rhetoric suffusing the various campaigns to annex and "free" Cuba from Spanish tyranny. Don Jorge, jubilant over his ill-gotten fortune, blithely denounces his "hot-headed [Cuban] compatriots" and their false "talk of love for their native land." In the final scenes, Lippard also revises the largely passive role of his working-class female heroine. Unlike the tragic Ophelia of *Charles Anderson Chester*, Kate lives to confront the Philadelphia merchants with proof damning them for participating in the illegal foreign slave trade in Cuba, and flees with Elijah to Panama, the cosmopolitan entrepôt and gateway to the fabled goldfields of the American West. As in *The Quaker City*, Lippard resolves the plot of this family melodrama in a vision of the as yet uncorrupted western territories. Their triumph is both financial and ethical, effected first by blackmailing Hicks's wealthy Philadelphia associates with proof of their participating in the illegal foreign slave trade in Cuba and then, it is implied, handing that proof over to the federal government.

This republication of *The Killers* contributes to current efforts to revitalize George Lippard for a new generation of readers. In 1855, a biography published shortly after Lippard's death (and assumed to be the work of John Bell Bouton, editor of the *Plain*

Dealer newspaper in Cleveland, Ohio) likened his literary craft to "the earnest skillful work of the dissecting-knife—the faithful laying bare of black hearts and oppressive institutions." "He thought of these wrongs," it continues, and "[w]ith scorn, and wrath, and execrations he flung defiance in their face, and shouted a battle-cry over the dumb anguish of the millions perishing in conventional lies."[87] In this iconoclastic spirit, *The Killers'* critique of corrupt Philadelphia banking establishments charts the uneven flows of global finance capital, and its squalid account of working-class tenement life reveals the interrelation of urbanization, industrial capitalism, and foreign immigration in the American city. In the novella, Lippard points to the generational continuities between slave-trading fathers and race-rioting sons, by situating, according to Otter, "the events that occur on a discrete Philadelphia night in systems of commerce that extend across the eastern seaboard and into the Caribbean."[88] He speaks to the ambiguities and contradictions of foreign relations in the formation of national culture, ongoing concerns in our ever-changing, interconnected world, and key analytics in the transnational and hemispheric turn in American studies. A wildly popular and polarizing figure in his day, Lippard continues to be one of the most underappreciated of major American writers. Written toward the end of his literary life, *The Killers* reveals a honed political aesthetic that centers racial discourse and proletarian struggles within an expanded critique of modern finance capitalism and its speculative culture founded on the transatlantic slave trade. At the end, the notorious Irish Catholic gang from which Lippard derives the novella's sensationalized title—and on whose morality he had focused in the shorter pamphlet version of the work—disappears from view. In its place, Lippard turns to the bankers, priests, and judges he calls the "Respectable Killers," as he transforms a gritty tale of urban gang violence into revolutionary political allegory. The "relentless foe of kingcraft, priestcraft, and a mere moneyed aristocracy," Lippard defied literary and social conventions, and his political critiques remain as prescient today as they were more than 150 years ago, foreshadowing the Occupy Wall Street movement and its unifying slogan of "We are the 99 percent."[89]

NOTE ON THE TEXT

In the absence of sales or distribution records, it is difficult to know which version of Lippard's novella saw the largest circulation in its time. No manuscript of the work is known to exist. But because the text—originally in columns in the Saturday newspaper the *Quaker City*—appears to have been produced from the same setting, put into different forms for the book versions *The Killers* and *The Bank Director's Son*, the codex version of *The Killers* (though, like *Charles Anderson Chester*, published anonymously and bearing a nonexistent publishing house on its title page) serves reasonably well as a source. The only differences among the versions that we have found are in the front matter of the bound versions and the introduction to the serialized version. The former have been reproduced as figures, and the latter appears transcribed in Appendix 2. Before the body of the text of *Life and Adventures of Charles Anderson Chester*, an interior title reads, "The Life and Exploits of Charles Anderson Chester"; we have chosen to refer to the text as a whole by its copyrighted title *Life and Adventures of Charles Anderson Chester*.

With the exceptions of line endings and pagination, we have chosen a diplomatic approach to reproducing the text, both to preserve some of the feel of the original and because the irregularities—some of spelling ("develope" or "carcase," for example) and others of punctuation (in contractions such as "have'nt," or the use of dashes, or the occasional dropped period)—are still comparatively undistracting. Also, Lippard is reported to have been a quick composer, with little enthusiasm for careful copyediting; presenting the text as closely as it appears in the original may help preserve a sense of the production mood of the novella. Where there was some risk of a lack of clarity, however, we have added a note with our best guess about the intended word or phrasing. We have employed the same policy with respect to the materials in the appendices.

The following sources were consulted for the copy and reproductions included here: at the Historical Society of Pennsylvania, *The Killers*, in the *Quaker City*, issues of December 1, 8, 15, 22, and 29, 1849; and at the Library Company of Philadelphia, *The Killers: A Narrative of Real Life in Philadelphia* (Philadelphia: Hankinson and Bartholomew, 1850); *Life and Adventures of Charles Anderson Chester, the Notorious Leader of the Philadelphia "Killers": Who Was Murdered, While Engaged in the Destruction of the California House, on Election Night, October 11, 1849* (Philadelphia: Yates and Smith, 1849); and George Lippard, *The Bank Director's Son, a Real and Intensely Interesting Revelation of City Life* (Philadelphia: E. E. Barclay and A. R. Orton, 1851). The reading texts of both *The Killers* and *Life and Adventures of Charles Anderson Chester* were prepared by Nicole H. Gray.

(facing page)
Figure 7. Cover.

George Lippard, *The Killers: A Narrative of Real Life in Philadelphia* (Philadelphia: Hankinson and Bartholomew, 1850). Am 1850 Lip. Courtesy of the Historical Society of Pennsylvania.

THE KILLERS.

A NARRATIVE

OF

REAL LIFE IN PHILADELPHIA,

*In which the deeds of the Killers, and the great Riot of election night, October 10, 1849,
are minutely described. Also, the adventures of three notorious individuals, who took
part in that Riot, to wit:*

CROMWELL D. Z. HICKS, *the Leader of the Killers,*

DON JORGE, *one of the Leaders of the Cuban Expedition, and*

"THE BULGINE," *the celebrated Negro Desperado of Moyamensing.*

BY A MEMBER OF THE PHILADELPHIA BAR.

PHILADELPHIA:
PUBLISHED BY HANKINSON AND BARTHOLOMEW.
1850.

THE KILLERS

PART I. THE STUDENTS.

On a warm summer night, in the year 1846, two students of Yale College, were sitting alone, in their room, in the —— Hotel, well known to the people of the fair City of Elms.[1] One of these young men was the son of a Philadelphia Merchant; the other was the son of a native of Cuba, who for political offences had been exiled from the "Gem of the Gulf." Seated near a table, copiously overspread with the tokens of student-life, in all its phases—pipes, cigars, bottles, glasses, Greek Grammars and Latin Lexicons—these young men were discussing their Havannahs[2] of the latest and best brand, as they engaged in earnest conversation.

Cromwell Hicks, the son of the Philadelphia merchant, was a youth of some nineteen years, rather tall, with blue eyes, fair complexion and a prominent chin adorned by a precocious beard. Dressed in a flashy wrapper, which thrown back, displayed a white vest and blue cravat, Cromwell rested his feet upon the table, in a manner that gave his comrade every opportunity to examine the plaid of his pantaloons and the patent leather of his gaiters.

The young Cuban was a man of different make: Slim, elegantly formed, his eyes, beard and complexion dark, he rested his elbows upon the table and leaning his cheeks upon his hands, looked steadily into the face of Cromwell from the opposite side of the table, at the same time passing the smoke of his cigar through his nostrils with all the gusto of a confirmed smoker. DON JORGE MARIN was two years older than his companion; and altogether of a more nervous and excitable temperament.

The conversation of the young men will disclose a portion of the incidents which open our narrative.

"Expelled!" said Cromwell with an emphatic puff.

"Expelled!" echoed Don Jorge, in very good English, and with a column of smoke issuing from each nostril.

"And after I have only been six months at College!" said Cromwell, helping himself to a glass of brandy.

"I have been here a little longer—a year," responded Don Jorge, lighting a fresh cigar.

"Just look at our affairs! In a lark—a quiet genteel sort of lark— we attempted to abduct the daughter of one of the Professors—after which, with an old cannon, we took a shy at one of the college buildings. We merely wished to have a little fun with the girl and blow the college building into its original element. And for this we have been expelled. Really George, my boy, the world is getting illiberal.

"What shall we do?" responded Jorge or George as you may choose to spell it—"I can't move until I get a letter from my father who is now at Saratoga.[3] You know he was exiled from Cuba when I was but a child, and since then we have subsisted upon the wreck of his fortune, which he managed to bring with him to this country. Funds are rather low with him just now, and besides that he is always engaged upon some attempt or other to free our native Island from the Spaniard. Besides he's rather indignant about some of my capers in New York last winter —"

Don Jorge was interrupted by his companion—

"I too am waiting for a letter from my father. He's an elderly gentleman, round in face and white in cravat—devoted to stocks— and with a kind of Quaker kink to the collar of his coat. Fond of good living—sometimes liberal—and sometimes stingy as Astor.[4] Mother, however, is my friend at court—some fifteen years younger than father, she always manages to bring the old man to terms. It was through her that I escaped the counting-room, and came to College. Zounds! I wish the letter would come."

Young Hicks rose, and going to the window looked out upon the night. It was hot, damp and "drizzly." A misty cloud overspread the City of Elms, and the prospect was cheerless as the young man's fortunes. While the young American, hands in his pockets, was engaged in a sort of vacant survey of the state of the weather, the young Cuban drew a letter from his pocket, postmarked "Saratoga," and signed "Antonio Marin." While he perused the letter a singular smile gleamed over his dark features, and his eyes shone with a sudden and peculiar light.

"I have heard from my father," he muttered, and replaced the letter in his vest pocket.

"Suppose the answer of your father is unfavorable, what will you do, Crom?" asked Don Jorge, as his comrade again approached the light—"Get a clerkship in Pearl street, or take daguerreotypes?"

The expression of his mustached lip did not altogether please Cromwell. He consigned the clerkship and the daguerreotype to a personage not to be mentioned, and rounding off the sentence with an oath continued—

"The old man dare not send an unfavorable letter. Mother won't let him."

Dropping into the chair, he took a fresh cigar, and in a moment was lost in a cloud.

"I wonder if all the servants have gone to bed? I should like to have some more brandy," exclaimed Don Jorge pulling the bell rope. In a moment—it did not seem longer—a servant appeared—and rubbing his sleepy eyelids, asked in good Hibernian—

"What 'ud yez plase to have Misther Hicks?"

"A little more brandy Patrick, and by the bye, I came in late, and had no chance to see whether there was any letters for me at the Bar. Do you know of any?"

"Letthers? Be jabers ye'll excuse me for saying the same but the Landlord was growlin' about your bill—a matther of three months unpaid—and the washerwoman was in the hall, all the night long, awaitin' yez and swarin' like blazes about the number of dozens that she's done for yez. And the tailor—fax if I was yez Misther Hicks I'd pay the divils and lave this afore they would say Jack Robinson—"

Patrick was the confidential servant of Mr. Cromwell Hicks—familiar with his vices and his money—hence his familiarity. On the present occasion however his jocular remarks uttered in the richest Hibernian, were received by his master with a gloomy scowl.

"Get some brandy Pat, and let the landlord, washerwoman and tailor go to the —— There were no letters left for me?"

A look of intelligence passed between the servant and Don Jorge. Patrick advanced to the light, searching in his pockets with a sort of half confused and half repentant air—

"Letthers! Och the blazes! Have I lost it?"

"Lost it?"

"Jist five minutes ago, there was a ring at the door, and one of the ould boys wid a white towel about his neck—one of the chaps from the college I mane—hands me a letther for you. Fax I'd not forgot it. Here's the crathur—"

Cromwell seized the letter, "From the old man!" he muttered and broke the seal. As he read Don Jorge watched him with a steady gaze. The countenance of young Hicks gradually darkened; his lip trembled, and at length flinging the letter across the table, he asked his companion to read it. Jorge seized the letter, and hastily gathered its contents:

SIR:

Your education, supposed to have been commenced at the counting room, but in reality begun at the race course, the bar room and the brothel, has I perceive found its appropriate termination in your recent exploits at college. You can now apply what you have learned, in your intercourse with the world. You will need all your knowledge, for as regards money, you need expect none from me. I have paid for your vices long enough and am determined to be disgraced by you no longer.

Yours, &c.

JACOB D. Z. HICKS.

P. S. This time the persuasions of your mother are fruitless. I have made up my mind.

When Jorge had finished the perusal of this fatherly epistle, he drew from his vest pocket the letter postmarked "Saratoga" and flung it across the table.

"Read it Crom. I received it this evening but was afraid to show it, until I learned your fate."

Cromwell cast his eye over the letter. It was brief and delightfully concise.

DON JORGE:

Degenerate son of an illustrious line, I have disowned you. I will pay none of your bills. You have nothing to expect from me. My parting advice is, that you lay aside the name which you have disgraced, and let me never hear from you again.

Adieu

ANTONIO MARIN.

Patrick who had observed the faces of the young gentlemen, with one eye closed, now broke the silence by the exclamation—

"It strikes me that there's a pair of yez in the same box, be jabers!"

This lively remark was answered by Cromwell with a sign and a word. He flung his book at the servant's head, adding significantly as he pointed to the door—"brandy!"

Patrick gone, the two young gentlemen took council together. Their condition was indeed desperate. Young, vigorous and with tolerable talents, they were ashamed to work, and had no disposition to earn its wages by one effort of honest toil. Educated in the bar-room, the gambling hell and the brothel, they now saw the world before them, and had the opportunity of testing its qualities, without a dollar in their pockets.

"Bad!" said Jorge, stroking his black mustache.

"Not a dollar!" responded Cromwell, and laid his head upon his hands. Patrick returned with the brandy and a bundle of cigars; after he had gone the young gentlemen took a glass of the former, and a couple of the latter, and set them down to contemplate their ruined fortunes. For a long time they drank and smoked in silence.

"I have it," cried Jorge, striking the table with his clenched hand. "You must go to Philadelphia—I to Saratoga. Each of us must have a talk with his father. In three days we'll meet in New York, at Lovejoy's Hotel[5] opposite the Park, and compare at once our finances and our prospects. Will you give me your hand on it?"

Cromwell opened his blue eyes,—"Why I have not a dollar to pay my passage from here to Philadelphia. I'm dead broke!"

Jorge displayed a twenty dollar bill—"I borrowed it from Patrick this afternoon. I'll halve it with you."

"But how can we leave the hotel without paying our bills?"

"Walk away," responded Jorge.—"Walk away at dead of night, Crom., and let the landlord wait until we are in funds."

"But suppose I come back to New York without a cent of money? Suppose the old man comes the granite—what then? Fathers have done such things?"

His eyes fiery with brandy, he awaited the answer of his comrade in evident hesitation. Don Jorge bent over the table, his dark features glowing with excitement.

"There is an island in the gulf—" he said; "an Eden of a place, with many a snug cove to shelter a craft which has not been properly cleared at the Custom House. You take? An Island which has free air, tropical fruits and flowers, aye and a grand old cove, just deep enough and wide enough, to shelter a band of brave fellows, who after the perils of the sea, may choose to solace their solitude with good wine and beautiful Creoles. Are you dull of comprehension, or shall I sing it for you?"

The excitement which animated his face seemed gradually to communicate itself to the fair complexioned visage of his friend.

"An island in the gulf? Bah! You ain't romancing? How shall we get there?"

"Four days from this a vessel leaves New York city for Turk's Island. Her papers are made out—her crew picked—her owners only wait my answer."

"Your answer?"

"Yes, *my answer*. Aware that I am by birth a Cuban, they seem to think that I can manage the affairs of the craft with the skill of a born sailor. I have been at sea, you know? These owners only wait for the captain and first mate of the "Sarah Jane." I have some knowledge of the sea; you have a steady eye, and firm nerves. I will be captain—you will be first mate—"

The proposition seemed to the half-drunken Philadelphian like the fancy of a dream.

"Pshaw! You aint in earnest? The days of Piracy are past and gone. As for Pirates, they only exist in Melo-dramas—particularly at the Chatham Street Theatre.[6] Come, Georgy, my boy, none of your gammon—"

"Piracy! I said nothing of Piracy," quietly interposed the Cuban, knocking the ashes from his cigar—"Just hand me the bottle, and I'll be more explicit."

The bottle was handed, glasses filled, and in a low voice Don Jorge began to develope his ideas. The countenance of Cromwell began to brighten with something more than drunken excitement.

"No! no! By Heaven, I'll have nothing to do with it," he cried, his not unhandsome face stamped with horror.

"But the one trip will set us up for life," persuasively suggested Don Jorge.

"I won't, I swear I won't!" fairly shrieked Cromwell—"Sooner will I go to Philadelphia and go into the Counting house as an errand boy. Come—George—this *is* a joke of yours—aint it now?"

The sombre visage of the Cuban fairly glistened with scorn. His lip curled under its dark mustache as he replied—

"If you had the heart or pluck of a man, you'd soon see what kind of a joke it is. I'm ashamed of you, Mr. Hicks."

These words excited all that was irritable in the heart of the young Philadelphian. Starting from his chair, he in incoherent words demanded an explanation from Don Jorge, and flung back the charge of cowardice into his teeth. The Cuban also rose, his countenance displaying more resolution than anger.

"It will do us no good to fight. Meet me three days from this, at Lovejoy's in New York, and if you don't conclude to accept my proposition, then I will fight you. There's my hand on it."

Young Hicks could not refuse the proffered hand.

In a few moments, the young gentlemen left the room and the hotel, without one word of farewell to the landlord.

Scarce had they gone, when Patrick entered their room, and surveying their trunks which locked and corded stood near the windows, he soliloquized: "Sure that Don Jorge is a broth of a boy! To go and pay the hotel bill and then purtend to stale off like a thafe o' th' world! An' it's my private opinion that he's got young Misther Hicks in tow, for some devl'ment or 'tother. Then he pays well, and it's a good five dollar bill this?'" drawing a bill from his pocket—"The blackguards! Div'l a drop in the bottle!"

—While Patrick concludes his soliloquy, and our two young gentlemen are pushing their way through the dark streets of New Haven, we will briefly inform the reader of one or two facts, which have an important bearing upon the course of this narrative.

Don Jorge had involved Crom. Hicks in the "scrape" which produced their expulsion. Don Jorge had written under an assumed name a full account of the affair to the father of his comrade. Don Jorge had himself written the letter, signed with the name of his own father, and contrived that it should be forwarded to him from Saratoga.

From this it will appear that Don Jorge had rather a deep interest in the affairs of Mr. Cromwell Hicks, son of Jacob D. Z. Hicks, Esq.

The nature of this interest will appear in the course of our narrative.

PART II. MR. CROMWELL HICKS
AND THE "OLD MAN."

Two days after the scene recorded in part I. late in the afternoon, Mr. Cromwell Hicks ascended the marble steps of his father's mansion in Walnut street. Dressed in a light blue frock, buff vest and plaid pants, Cromwell was covered with the dust of the cars; and his whole appearance betrayed the tokens of anxiety and fatigue. His heart fluttering under his buff vest, he pulled the bell. It was answered by a strange servant, who answered his inquiry in regard to his father, with the information that Mr. Hicks and family had left four days previous for Cape May.[7]

This was an unexpected blow. Surveying first the vacant face of the servant, and then casting a glance at his dusty attire, Cromwell for a few moments was in doubt as to his future course. It was a broiling day; the streets were almost deserted; to his eye the town looked black and gloomy as in mid-winter. He was without a dollar in the world, having spent the last cent in defraying his passage from New York.

"Will you leave your name, sir?" asked the servant.

"Never mind," exclaimed Cromwell, "I'll stop at the counting house and leave my message with Mr. Grimly."

The "counting house" was an old brick building, which stood in an alley near Chesnut and Front, amid warehouses of more modern construction, beside which it looked like an old fashioned "man of business," dressed in Quaker garb, compared with the high collared and dapper built men of business of the present day. It was antiquity itself. Its bricks were faded, its windows small and dark, its cellars deep and cavernous: it was in fact one of the old houses belonging to old firms, which do more business in one day, with all their cobwebs and dust, than your modern house does in a year. To this aged edifice, determined to try his powers of persuasion upon Mr. Grimly, his father's head clerk, Cromwell bent his steps.

He entered the counting room. It was hidden away at the farther end of a large gloomy place, and was fenced off from bales of goods, and hogsheads of cogniac,[8] by a dingy railing of unpainted pine.

"Where is Mr. Grimly?" asked young Hicks, of the negro porter, who was the only person visible.

"Jist gone out," answered the porter, who did not recognize his employer's son; "back d'rectly."

The Killers

"I'll wait for him," was the answer, and Cromwell sauntered into the counting room, which was furnished with an old chair, a large desk and a range of shelves filled with ledgers. It was a gloomy place, with a solitary window looking out upon a gloomier yard. An opened letter, spread upon the desk, attracted the eye of the hopeful youth. It was from Cape May, bore the signature of his father, was addressed to Mr. Grimly his head clerk, and contained this brief injunction:

"Grimly—I send you a check for $5,000. Cash it, and meet that note of Tompkins & Co.—to-morrow—you understand?"

"Where the deuce is the check?" soliloquised Cromwell, and forthwith began to look for it, but in vain. While thus engaged, his ear was attracted by the sound of a footstep. Looking through the railing, he beheld a short, little man, with a round face and a hooked nose, approaching at a brisk pace. As he saw him, his fertile brain hit upon a plan of operation.

"Grimly, my good fellow," he said, as the head clerk opened the door of the counting room, "I've been looking for you all over town. Quick!—At Walnut street wharf!—There's no time to be lost!"

He spoke these incoherent words with every manifestation of alarm and terror. As much surprised at the sudden appearance of the vagabond son in the counting room, as at his hurried words, the head clerk was for a few moments at a loss for words.

"You here—umph! Thought you was at College—eh!" exclaimed Grimly as soon as he found his tongue—"Walnut street wharf? What *do* you mean?"

"Mr. Grimly," responded the young man slowly and with deliberation, "I mean that in returning from Cape May father has been stricken with an apoplectic fit. He's on board the boat. Mother

[58]

sent me up here, to tell you to come down without delay. Quick! No time's to be lost."

Grimly seemed thunderstricken. He placed his finger on the tip of his nose, muttering—"Old Hicks struck with apoplexy—bad! bad! Here's this check to be cashed, and that note of Tompkins & Co. to be met. What shall I do—"

"I'll tell you, Grimly. Give me the check—I'll get it cashed and then go and take up the note, while you hurry down to the wharf."

He said this in quite a confidential manner, laying his hand on Grimly's arm and looking very affectionately into his face.

In answer to this, Mr. Grimly closed one eye—arranged his white cravat—and seemed buried in thought, while Cromwell stood waiting with evident impatience for his answer.

"You've been to Cape May—have you?" he said, regarding Cromwell with one eye closed.

"You know I haven't. I have just got on from New York, and met one of father's servants as I was coming off the boat. He told me the old gentleman had been taken with apoplexy on the way up. I went into the cabin of the Cape May boat which had just come to, and saw father there. Mother gave me the message which I have just delivered. Indeed, Mr. Grimly you'd better hurry—"

"Then you had better take this check," said Grimly extending his hand, "Get it cashed and take up that note. It is now half past two, it must be done without delay."

His eyes glistening Cromwell reached forth his hand to grasp the check, when Mr. Grimly drew back his hand, quietly observing at the same time "I think Cromwell you had better ask your father. Here he is. Rather singular that he's so soon recovered from his fit of apoplexy?"

Scarcely had the words passed his lips, when at his shoulder appeared the portly figure of the father, Mr. Jacob D. Z. Hicks, a gentleman of some fifty years, dressed in black with a white waistcoat. His ruddy face was overspread with a scowl; he regarded his son with a glance full of meaning, at the same time passing his 'kerchief incessantly over his bald crown. He had overheard the whole of the conversation between his son and his head clerk. He had indeed returned from Cape May, but had seen his clerk, *only five minutes previous to this interview*. His feelings as he overheard the conversation may be imagined.

"Scoundrel!" was his solitary ejaculation, as he gazed upon his son, who now stood cowering and abashed, in one corner of the counting room.

"Father—" hesitated Cromwell.

The merchant pointed to the door.

"Go!" he said, and motioned with his finger.

"Forgive me, father—I've been wild. I know it—" faltered Cromwell.

"You saw me in a fit, did you? And you would have got that check cashed and taken up Tompkins & Co's note—would you? You're a bigger scoundrel than I took you for. Go!"

Cromwell moved to the door. While the head clerk stood thunderstricken, the father followed his son into the large room, which filled with hogsheads and bales, intervened between the counting room and the street. Cromwell quietly threaded his way through the gloomy place, and was passing to the street when his father's hand stopped him on the threshold.

"Cromwell," said he, "let us understand one another."

Cromwell turned with surprise pictured on his face, the

countenance of his father was fraught with a meaning which he could not analyze.

"In the first place," said the Merchant, "Read this."

He handed his son a copy of the New York Herald dated the day previous. The finger of Mr. Jacob D. Z. Hicks pointed a paragraph embodied in a letter from Cape May. Cromwell read in silence, his face displaying every change of incredulity succeeded by surprise.

"By the bye you have heard that a distinguished scion of the British Aristocracy, who passes under the title of Sir Charles Wriothelsy has been figuring rather extensively at this place. The Baronet is a gallant gentleman, with a pale mouse colored mustache and aristocratic air.—He has excited quite a sensation. He is altogether a man of ton[9]—elegant and fascinating, so much so, that yesterday the young wife of one of our old Philadelphia merchants was detected in a rather embarrassing situation with the gallant Briton, and worst of all, the discoverer was her venerable spouse. The affair has created a great talk. To-morrow I will send you full particulars."

"Well—what of this?" said Cromwell, looking into his father's face.

"Nothing much. Only that young wife of an old merchant, was your mother. I married her at sixteen; married her out of regard for her family, and have lived with her these nineteen years. She is now about thirty-four, but as young and lively as ever. The day-before yesterday she disgraced me at Cape May, and strengthened a resolve which I have long indulged, to wit, to cast her and her son to the winds, or the d—l. You comprehend, Cromwell! You are not my son. The conduct of your mother breaks all ties between us. (By the bye I may remark that yesterday she eloped with her Baronet.) For nineteen years I have supported you. You can gamble, drink and act the gentleman in every way. Your education is complete. My advice to you, is, to follow your mother, who yesterday eloped with her British Baronet. From me, from this hour, you can expect nothing. Beg, starve or steal—as you please—do it in a gentlemanly way if you like—but from me you shall never receive one cent. We understand one another. Good day Sir."

With these words the old man turned away, leaving Cromwell pale and thunderstricken on the threshold. The thunderbolt which had fallen upon him, deprived him for the time of all control over his reason.

At last, still holding the New York Herald in his hand, he took his way from the store of his *late* father. As he passed along the alley into Front street, he tried—for a long time without success—to realize his situation. His mother a disgraced woman—himself pronounced an illegitimate by the man whom he had always known as his father—he could not believe it. But the New York Herald was in his hands, the words of the old Merchant still rang in his ears. Then, when he contrasted the youth of his mother with the age of her husband, her fondness for admiration and show with the sedate and rather old fashioned habits of the Merchant, the story appeared more reasonable. A thousand things came to the memory of Cromwell, which seemed to confirm the story of Mr. Jacob Hicks. Suffice it to say, that after an hour's walk up and down the street, Cromwell found himself at the corner of Second and Walnut street, with three facts impressed rather vividly upon his mind; He was without a father; his mother had eloped with a mustache (appended to a

British Baronet;) and he, Cromwell Hicks, late of Yale College, was without a cent in the world.

PART III. THE LETTER
OF THE DISHONORED WIFE.

Here let us leave the son for a few hours, while we attend to his father. After Mr. Jacob D. Z. Hicks had delivered his mind to Cromwell, his supposed son, he turned from the door and retreated within the white pine railing of his counting room.

"Mr. Grimly," he said to his head clerk, "to-night we will receive by the Southern mail from five to six thousand dollars, in sight drafts[10] upon New York. You will open the letters and attend to these drafts if you please. We are rather hard up for cash now, and will need all the money we can rake and scrape to meet our engagements."

Mr. Grimly said a few words in acquiescence, and then retired, leaving the Merchant alone in the counting room.

That gentleman seated himself on the high stool with his back against the wall—folded his arms—projected his nether lip—and for an instant seemed wrapt in a brown study.

A few words may throw some light upon the character of Mr. Hicks. He was not a bad man. He was not a Merchant, nor a Banker, nor a Broker; he was a combination of the three. He was that embodiment of inimitable energy, and grasping meanness, which in modern days is called a "business man." Mr. Hicks was by birth a Quaker, and yet he was also a nominal member of the Episcopal church. Not that he particularly believed in that church, or held much faith in any church. Possibly, after this "business world" there might be a hereafter; and Mr. Hicks thought it no harm to be on the safe side.

The great object of Mr. Hicks was to make money. The religion of his life was to increase his power among men of money.

Did he spend this money in the gratification of his appetites? We cannot tell.

No one knew how much Mr. Hicks was worth. His father had been very rich: his wealth—such was the popular rumor—had been acquired in the slave trade at a time when the slave trade was as legal, moral and religious, as stock gambling at the present day. Although no one knew how much Mr. Hicks was worth, his wealth was never rated below $200,000 in real estate. Then he had an interest in two or three country banks; he was largely concerned in the stock market; he was also something of a politician.

Now, as Mr. Hicks sat alone in his counting room, his thoughts mingled the sweet with the bitter, in almost equal quantities.

"I don't care about her intimacy with the Baronet. The publicity of the thing galls me. For that matter, I've known her real character since the day when I married her to hide her shame, and have winked at her frequent partialities for gentlemen with mustaches—musical gentlemen and gentlemen of the stage. I hate the talk and fuss which will be made all over town about this matter, but at the same I'm glad she's gone. And then her beautiful boy is off my hands. That's some comfort. I am now alone in the world, and will only have to 'look out' for myself."

Mr Hicks drew from a side pocket a letter which he had that day received from his unfaithful spouse. He had broken the seal but had not read it.

"Sentiment, I 'spose—chock full of sentiment," he muttered, as he opened the letter and held it toward the window—"Romantic talk about the 'bruised heart,' the 'disparity of age,' and what not. It's full of such stuff I 'spose."

But somewhat to his surprise the letter was altogether of a different character. The reader may glean some ideas of the fugitive lady from the epistle which follows:

HICKS:

There's no use of any nonsense between us. You know *why* you married me nearly nineteen years ago. You know what kind of a life we have led together—you pursuing your own way, and I mine, these eighteen years. However, as I have something important to communicate to you, you will suffer me to recapitulate.

At the time when we first met, I had just turned sixteen. I was the daughter of one of the oldest and wealthiest families in Philadelphia—you know that I was good looking—and was therefore caressed, flattered, idolized. Among the gentlemen who came to my father's house were yourself, a very plain business sort of man; and a very handsome foreigner, who was connected with the French Embassy at Washington, and who carried the word "Count" before his name. You wished to marry me because I was rich, and because yourself (although reputed to be rich) were on the verge of bankruptcy, notwithstanding the reputed fortune left you by your father. The Count could not marry me because he had a wife living in France; but this did not prevent me from becoming very painfully involved with that

gentleman. My father discovered my situation soon after the
Count had suddenly left for France. And my father, who
knew of your embarrassments, proposed the match between
you and I—stating *all* the circumstances to you—and you
gladly consented. We were married. We immediately
left the country, in order to spend the first months of our
marriage in Paris. Here my Cromwell was born: he passed
in the eyes of the world as your son; while both of us knew
the real facts of the case. So conscious was you that he was a
sort of usurper on the rights of your *future* children that you
named him "CROMWELL."[11] A few months after his birth
we returned to Philadelphia; and almost a year afterward
your son was born. This occurred while you were absent
from the city—absent in the West on a business tour. When
you returned, myself and the doctor informed you that the
second child (that is yours) had died a few moments after its
birth. You were shown its coffin in the family vault.

Now I've a sort of confession to make to you, which I
don't make from any sentimental idea of repentance and
all that sort of thing, but because I really wish to do you a
service. That second child did not die. He is now living.
For eighteen years or so I have secretly contributed to his
support. "For the facts of the case" (as the newspapers say)
listen.

The second child, soon after its birth, was entrusted
to the care of a friend of the nurse, who brought it up as
her own, and who has received from me, for these eighteen
years, the quarterly sum of sixty dollars. This friend of
the nurse goes by the name of Mrs. Watson; she is the wife

of a drunken fellow; and lives in Runnel's Court, in the neighborhood of Sixth and South streets. Your son was living under her roof three months ago, when I paid the last quarterly instalment. I don't know—have never desired to know his name. To-morrow the quarterly instalment should again be paid. Mrs. Watson will expect it. Had you not better attend to it?

You will doubtless enquire my motive for having your own child taken out of sight, while I brought up mine in its place, in your house, as your son. I knew very well, that your child would have been petted and favored, while mine would have been insulted and neglected. You could not have borne Cromwell before your sight, while your own child was in the house. The course which I pursued relieved me from a great deal of trouble, and spared you the pain of making an eternal comparison between the first child who has *noble blood* in his veins, and the second child, who is only a—Hicks.

Now, I well know that you will not dare to cast off Cromwell; fear of the world's talk will prevent you from doing such a foolish thing. At the same time, I tell you all about your own child, and advise you to see Mrs. Watson, without delay. You will receive this at the time when Sir Charles and myself will be on our way to Montreal, where we intend to spend the summer and fall. I ask nothing from you, for myself, as my father before his death secured a very pretty fortune to me, in my own name.

Hicks, adieu,

JULIA CORNELIA HICKS.

Mr. Hicks read the letter and his face displayed all the changes of the kaleidoscope. He was not much given to a display of his feelings, but when he came to the line which announced the existence of his own child, he turned pale as death, and felt his heart contract within him, as though suddenly compressed with the jaws of a vice. After he had finished the epistle from his profligate wife, he sat for at least five minutes, gazing upon the letter with a vacant stare. Could Cromwell have seen him at this moment, he would have been amply revenged for the scene of an hour previous. At length, in some measure recovering his presence of mind, Hicks slid from his seat, and hurrying through the store, confronted Mr. Grimly, who had just returned from the post office.

"Tom has not returned from the post office," said Mr. Grimly—"I have just been down there, and cannot see any letters in the box. Tom has been gone a good while—what can it mean?"

At any other time these words would have arrested the attention of Mr. Hicks, but now brushing past his head clerk, with an "I'm in a hurry, Grimly," he made his way along the alley towards Front street.

"I'll see this Mrs. Watson," he muttered—"See her at once—to-night—and see for myself what kind of boy this is. I can acknowledge him for my own or not, just as I please."

The letter of the abandoned wife had raised something like the feeling of paternity in the heart of the Merchant. Hurrying down Front street, he turned up South, and after much enquiry succeeded in finding "Runnel's Court."

PART IV. RUNNEL'S COURT.

Runnel's Court was one of those blots upon the civilization of the Nineteenth Century, which exist in the city and districts of Philadelphia, under the name of Courts. It extended between two narrow streets, and was composed of six three story brick houses built upon an area of ground scarcely sufficient for the foundation of one comfortable dwelling. Each of these houses comprised three rooms and a cellar. The cellar and each of the rooms was the abode of a family. And thus, packed within that narrow space, twenty-four families managed to exist, or rather to die by a slow torture, within the six houses of Runnel's Court. Whites and blacks, old and young, rumsellers and their customers, were packed together there, amid noxious smells, rags and filth, as thick and foul as insects in a decaying carcase.[12]

As Mr. Hicks entered the narrow pathway between the houses, (three of which facing the other three formed the court) he was nearly stifled by the hot and pestilential odors which accumulated in that wretched place.

"Where does Mrs. Watson live?" he asked; and was answered by a slatternly woman, who stood leaning against the door-post of a "groggery." (Understand, a groggery in a court is a kind of hell within a hell. The "court" itself is bad and foul enough, but the groggery completes the hideous scene, and makes it fit for the approbation of the Devil himself.)

"On the third flure," said the woman, pointing upwards, as she surveyed the dress of Mr. Hicks with a leer of drunken surprise. "She's a widdy now. Her husband fell off a buildin' about three months ago an' was kilt dead."

Mr. Hicks entered the house designated by the woman. Passing through the first and second rooms, (and through scenes of squalor and drunkenness that we have no wish to describe) he ascended into the room on the third floor. In a room about ten feet square, furnished with one table and two chairs, and lighted by two windows, one of which caught a gleam of the setting sun, sat a woman who might have been no more than forty years of age, though she looked sixty. Dressed in a gown of faded calico, her thin and "scrawny" neck surmounted by a face which looked haggard with premature age, if not with vice or hardship, this woman turned her dull eyeballs toward Mr. Hicks, as he entered her room, with a vague and almost idiotic stare.

"I can't pay it to-day," she mumbled, "Haint got the tin."

"My good woman," said Mr. Hicks, as he advanced with a bland smile—"You owe me nothing. I have merely called on a friendly visit. Allow me to ask, is your name Mrs. Watson?"

"It aint anything else, hoss," was the rather classic reply of the lady, who clutched in her colorless fingers a half-filled vial, on which Mr. Hicks read the word "Laudanum."[13]

"You have children?" asked Mr. Hicks, depositing himself on the unoccupied chair.

The woman looked at him with a glance in which stupidity seemed to struggle wtth suspicion.

"What's that your business?" she replied, and pulled her faded cap over a dingy brown wig, which but illy concealed her gray hair.

"Let me come to the point at once," resumed Mr. Hicks, "You have received for some years back the sum of sixty dollars per quarter?"

"I have that," and a light suddenly flashed in her leaden eyeballs.

"Do you know who it was that sent you this sum?"

"Blast me if I do. I only knew that it was due yesterday, and that it did not come."

"How was this sum usually sent to you?"

"I mostly got it through the post office—sometimes it was fetched to me by a person I did not know—" and she straightened herself in her chair, and began to look sternly into the merchant's face. "What do *you* know about it?"

"Just this. If you answer my questions satisfactorily, I will see myself that the same sum is paid to you in future, to wit, sixty dollars per quarter. The person who has been sending it to you died last night."

"Eh? You don't say! Well *now!* We're all but poor mortal creturs after all. Aint we?"

"How many children have you?"

"Kate and 'Lijah," sharply responded Mrs. Watson.

"How old is Kate, and what does she do?" asked Mr. Hicks, rubbing the perspiration from his glowing face, with a red bandanna.

"Kate is fourteen, and works in the Factory."

"And Elijah?" said Mr. Hicks rubbing his bald crown, with a great deal of zeal.

"'Lijah must be somethin' 'twixt eighteen and nineteen. But look here—what have you got to do with this business?"

"Where does Elijah work?"

"He was makin' shoes at the last accounts," said Mrs. Watson turning her face from the light.

"You have'nt seen him lately then. But where does he work?"

The woman seemed to hesitate. Her pallid lip trembled, while her eyes grew animated, almost brilliant.

"What's it your business?" she replied, turning her face to the wall.

"Why my good woman, I know that Elijah is not your son. I know that you received him some nineteen—perchance only eighteen years ago—from the hands of a Nurse, who kept secret the name of his mother. And further, I know that on your answers to my inquiries, depends your allowance of sixty dollars per quarter. Answer me plainly, is Elijah Watson dead?"

The woman turned her face toward the merchant. Her haggard features worked convulsively. Something like a tear struggled over her sallow cheeks.

"Lijah aint my son—that's true—but I've brought him up as mine, and like him just as well as Kate."

"But *where* is he?" asked Mr. Hicks, continuing the manual exercise of the handkerchief with great vigor.

The woman looked at him steadily, said one word, and burst into tears.

"In the Penitentiary," she said, and pointed with her colorless fingers to the north-west.

The Merchant recoiled as if appalled by the sight of an Apparition.

It was some time before he could resume the conversation. But when, in a tremulous voice, he again questioned the woman, he assured himself of the truth of two things. 1. That Elijah Watson was indeed his son. 2. That Elijah Watson was a convict in the eastern penitentiary.[14]

It was quite dark when he left the house of Mrs. Watson in Runnell's Court. He went directly home to his mansion in Walnut street, passed through those splendid rooms in which was neither wife nor child to welcome him, and locking himself in his chamber, thought all night of Elijah Watson and the Eastern Penitentiary.

PART V. MR. WHITELY THE BROKER.

While Mr. Jacob D. Z. Hicks tosses on his bed, and sees "PENITENTIARY" written on the black cloud of every dream, let us turn back in our narrative and take up the adventures of Cromwell.

We left him at the moment when, desolate and penniless, he stood in Walnut street, in the light of a declining summer day, pondering very seriously over the prospects of his future.

"I should be in New York to-night, and I haven't a fip to buy a cigar, much less four dollars to pay my passage."

He cast a glance over his apparel. Blue coat, plaid pants and buff vest looked remarkably dusty and travel-worn. He felt his pockets. They were deplorably empty. He looked up and down Walnut street, as the day began to decline over the town, and brought himself to the conclusion expressed in these words, muttered through his set teeth—"Without father or mother, friend or dollar, my chance of a bed and supper to-night gets dim and dimmer."

Again the thought then came over him, that he had promised to meet Don Jorge at Lovejoy's in New York on the third day from the period when they left New Haven together. This was the third day. How should he keep his appointment? He had not a dollar in the world to pay his fare to New York.

"And even if I can make out to get to New York to-night, nothing remains for me but to accept that cursed proposition."

In this mood he took his way toward the Exchange. He was roused from a reverie by a hand laid on his arm, and by the words, "How d'ye do, Mister Crom?"

Starting from his gloomy reverie, Cromwell beheld a youth of some fourteen years, whose turn-up nose and closely cut hair, together with corduroy pants and brown linen jacket, brought home to him the fact, that he beheld no less a personage than Mr. Tom Miller, who was employed in a double capacity—half as errand boy and half as under cleik[15]—in his father's store. Tom was delighted to see Cromwell—asked him when he had arrived in the city—how long he intended to stay—with other questions quite as interesting. As for Cromwell, quietly keeping his eye upon the youth, who held a package in his right hand, he said:

"Give me the letters, Tom. I'll take them down to the store. As for you, father wants you to go up to the Baltimore Depot, and bring down a box that is there, addressed to him. Just tell the agent that father sent you, and he'll give you the box. Mind that you hurry back."

Without a word the red-haired youth handed the letters to young Hicks, and hurried up Walnut street, on his way to Eleventh and Market. Cromwell slipped the letters into his pocket, gazed for a moment after the form of the errand boy, and then hurrying down Walnut street, turned into a "pot house," whose sign displayed tempting inducements to "sailors and emigrants." It was a miserable place, with one chair, a box, and a little man with a dirty face and one eye.

"What'll yes pleze to have, sur?"

Cromwell called for a glass of whiskey, and turning his back to the landlord, drew the package from his pocket, and proceeded to count the letters he had received from Tom. There were ten in all; one was particularly heavy; and all of them were carefully sealed. Did one, or did all of them contain money? This was an important question, but Cromwell did not choose to solve it in the pot house. But how shall he pay for the glass of whiskey? He had not a penny in the world. This placed him in a decidedly bad predicament. Waiting until the landlord had turned his back for a moment, Cromwell passed quietly from the place, and hurried up Walnut street, turned into Dock, and in a few moments was in Third street in the vicinity of Chesnut.

He had decided upon a difficult step. The letters which he held, bore the post-marks of distant parts of the Union, and very possibly they contained drafts upon houses in New York. It was his resolution to ascertain this fact in the first place, and in the second to get these drafts cashed. It was after bank hours, and only two broker's offices in the vicinity remained open. Cromwell's brain was in a whirl; conscious that whatever he did must be done without delay, he stood on the sidewalk, with his finger raised to his forehead, anxiously engaged in cogitating some scheme which might enable him to cash the drafts in the letters—that is, if said letters happened to contain drafts, or money in any shape.

But was this the case? Cromwell turned into an alley and with a trembling hand broke the seals of the letters. His hair reeled as their contents were disclosed to his gloating eyes. For those letters did contain drafts at one, two and three days sight, drawn upon certain firms in New York, and amounting altogether to five thousand and sixty dollars. Crumbling the letters, drafts and all into his pocket, Cromwell, staggered from the alley like a drunken man. He had resolved upon his course of action. Entering a small periodical agency, he called for pen and paper, and (while the boy in attendance was waiting upon a customer) our hero proceeded in quite a business-like manner to sign the name of "Jacob D. Z. Hicks" upon each of those talismanic slips of paper. Habit had made him familiar with his late father's signature; he wrote with ease and facility; in a few moments the work was done. He carefully sanded the signatures, and then made the best of his way to the office of a celebrated broker with whom his father had dealt for many years. On the threshold he paused; his heart beat like the pendulum of a clock; gazing through the glass door he beheld the familiar face of the Broker, bald head, high shirt collar, gold spectacles and all. For a moment the young gentleman hesitated; at length commanding all the force of his nerves, he entered, and opening the magic slips of paper upon the counter, said with great self-possession—"Mister Whitely, father starts for Niagara early in the morning. He would like it as a favor, if you would cash these drafts to-night."

The broker recognized young Hicks, addressed him by name, and after a word or two as to his father's health, examined the draft—first one side and then the other. This done, he paused, and surveyed Cromwell through his gold spectacles. Cromwell never forgot that scrutinizing gaze. "He suspects something," he muttered to himself, while in fact the worthy Broker, who was somewhat absent-minded, was cogitating whether or no he should ask as to the truth of that story about the Briton.

"Five thousand and sixty dollars," said the Broker.

"Can you do it?" gasped Cromwell, much agitated, but endeavoring to look as calm as possible.

"Certainly," was the answer—"would your father like city or New York funds?"[16]

"As you please," faltered Cromwell. "Only he wanted a thousand in twenties."

The Broker unlocked his iron safe and counted out five thousand and sixty dollars—forty $100 dollar bills and the balance in $20 notes—Cromwell watching him all the while with a feverish eye.

Young Hicks extended his hand, and could scarce believe the evidence of his senses when he felt the silken slips of paper between his fingers. He thrust them into his breast pocket and hurried to the door.

"Ah—come back, young man," he heard the voice of the broker.

It was the first impulse of the hopeful youth to put to his heels, but turning, with a pallid face, he again confronted the spectacled broker.

"Young man, that is, Mr. Hicks," began the Broker, "If it's not impolite I'd like to ask you one question."

Cromwell shook in "his boots" but managed to falter out the monosyllable, "Well?"

"Is there any truth in that story, eh—eh—about the Brit-British Baronet—and—" he paused.

Cromwell raised his handkerchief to his eyes, and in a voice broken by emotion, faltered—

"Mr. Whitely, a son should never speak of his mother's faults—" and as if overcome by his feelings hastened from the Broker's store.

Making the best of his way down Third, he struck into Dock street, and then turned down Walnut street. As he approached the corner of Front and Walnut streets, he heard the ringing of a bell. Utterly bewildered by the incidents of the last hour, he was hurrying at random—he knew not whither—when the ringing of the bell decided him, as to his future course.

"It's the New York bell!" he muttered, and in five minutes had purchased his ticket, and was on board the steamboat on his way to New York.

That night at ten he landed at the foot of Courtlandt street. Without pausing to eat or sleep, he proceeded to a Barber shop, and had his face cleanly shaved. Then, in an hour's ramble, he provided himself with a large trunk, a black wig, a pair of false whiskers, and two suits of clothes. He assumed the wig and whiskers in the street; put on a single-breasted frock coat, buttoning to the neck, in a tailor's store; covered his forehead with a glazed cap, and then calling a cab directed the driver to take his trunk to Lovejoy's Hotel.

PART VI. CROMWELL, DON JORGE AND THE POLICE OFFICER.

He entered his name on the books in a bold dashing hand—
"AUGUSTE BELAIR, *Montreal*."

Then seating himself in an arm chair, amid the noise and smoke of the reading room, he at once contemplated his black hair and whiskers, through the medium of a mirror, and endeavored to frame some plan, by which he might be enabled to decline both of Don Jorge's propositions. He had no desire to take the very honorable position of first mate on board of the Sara Jane. He was not decidedly anxious to fight his friend, either at fisticuffs or coffee and pistols. What should he do? With five thousand dollars in his pocket there came over the young gentleman's soul, a glorious and entrancing vision of Paris. Paris by day and by gaslight, Paris above ground and below!

"Yes, I'll cut the Sara Jane, and strike for Paris!" he said, half aloud—"At the age of nineteen and with five thousand in the pocket Paris will be interesting—most undoubtedly. Then I may chance to come across my "Ma" and her Baronet. Certainly I'll cut the Sara Jane."

But the young gentleman was not yet on board the Steamship, and there's many a slip between young gentlemen who sign other folk's names and the deck of a steamer.

A slim, dapper formed, dark whiskered gentleman passed between Cromwell and the mirror. It was Don Jorge. He did not recognize his friend. But it was no part of Cromwell's plan to avoid the young Cuban. So springing from his chair he greeted him with a familiar slap on the back, and said gaily—"I am true to my appointment. How are you, Don!"

It was some moments before Don Jorge could recognize his friend in the metamorphosed individual before him. At length the recognition was complete, and drawing their chairs into an obscure corner of the room, the friends began to compare notes. Don Jorge summed up the case for himself in a few words:

"I saw my father, spoke to him, and he would'nt even so much as recognize me. Here is nothing before me but the Sara Jane, and a trip from *you know where* to Brazil or Cuba."

What was his surprise, when Cromwell communicated the details of his last exploit! The eyes of the Cuban fairly danced with excitement. Cromwell had no reserves, and so he told him the entire story concluding with these words—

"So, with five thousand in my pocket, Georgy, there's no use of my having anything to do with the Sara Jane. The Steamer sails to-morrow; come along my boy. What say you? A trip to Paris?"

The head of the Spaniard dropped moodily upon his breast, and he shaded his eyes with his hand. Whether the sudden possession of five thousand disconcerted his plans, or not, we cannot tell, but after a few moments he spoke in a low, earnest voice, and compared the chances of Cromwell's arrest—did he once take passage on board the steamer—with the certainty of success and fortune, in case he linked his destiny with Don Jorge and the Sara Jane.

"Come! She lies anchored in the East River. I saw the owners not two hours ago and we must be off. Our baggage has been forwarded from New Haven, and you've only to say the word, and we'll move. Come."

He rose from his chair, and moved a step toward the door.

But Cromwell did not rise.

"No, S-i-r," he answered, cooly placing his feet upon the table, "You don't catch 'this child' in any scrape of that kind, while he has five thousand in his pocket—"

"Fool!" responded Don Jorge—"Why the very bank notes which you have about you will betray you. They will be advertised. You can't get them changed for gold or for English funds without the certainty of arrest."

Cromwell started from his chair, quietly buttoning his frock coat.

"I think you called me—fool?" he said, advancing to Don Jorge with a threatening air.

But ere Don Jorge could reply, a short personage who had been attentively reading a paper for some minutes past—at a distance of at least two yards from our worthies—suddenly turned, and tapping Cromwell on the shoulder—addressed him with the words—"You are my prisoner!"

Cromwell felt a shudder pervade him, as he surveyed the short personage, whose hat drawn low over the brow—and a "shocking bad hat" it was—did not altogether conceal a hangdog visage.

"Your prisoner!" echoed the hopeful youth, while Don Jorge stood regarding the two with calm satisfaction.

"I have watched you since you landed at Courtlandt street. That 'ere false wig and them false whiskers belong, in my humble opinion, to a suspicious character. You'd better come along. The Ma'or, or the chief o' poleese, 'ud be very much pleased to see you."

Cromwell lost color and nerve. Once before the Mayor, he would be searched—detained—and Mr. Jacob D. Z. Hicks would have time to come on from Philadelphia, and regain his money.

"Come, Mister," said the personage (who may have been a police officer, or a pickpocket, for all we know) when Don Jorge stepped between the pair.

"If I get you out of this scrape will you consent?" he whispered—"Say it quick, yes or no—"

Cromwell surveyed the ill-looking personage, and then faltered, "Yes!"

"Step this way, sir," he said, and the gentleman obeyed, still keeping his eye upon Cromwell—"Now, mark me, I know that you are an impostor, but for reasons of my own I choose to humor you. What do you charge for your impertinence? Name a reasonable sum, and let my friend go, and I'll pay it down—"

The fellow hesitated, and then with a leer meant to be very knowing, said—"Twenty dollars 'ill do it."

Don Jorge borrowed the twenty of Cromwell, paid it, and bade the fellow begone, with these words, which he uttered in a whisper—"Go! And if I see your face again I'll point you out to the police."

The personage seemed to understand, for he left the reading room in a hurry, while Cromwell stood silent and confused, a wondering spectator of the scene.

"We've no time to lose," said Don Jorge—"We must move right off. That fellow may be back in five minutes. Come, Crom. Hurrah for the Sara Jane, and—you know where!"

Crom. submitted like a child. Their trunks lashed behind a hack, and themselves seated within, they were whirling down Broadway in five minutes, at a speed which hackney coaches never attained before. In fifteen minutes they were at the Battery, where a boat was waiting for them. They entered, and through the clear starlight were rowed towards a bright light, which shone vividly at the distance of perchance five hundred yards. Up the deck of the Sara Jane, and into a luxuriantly furnished cabin—it was the work of five minutes more. And seated in chairs which were arranged beside a well furnished board, Cromwell and Don Jorge looked into each other's faces—the former silent and wondering, the latter gay and triumphant.

"Is it not a dream?" began Cromwell.

"Carlos," cried Don Jorge, and in answer a mulatto boy, dressed in livery, appeared. "Pen and paper," continued Don Jorge. The boy obeyed.

"Now, before we discuss our prospects over a bottle of this

wine, I want you, Crom, to write a letter to your father at my dictation."

The letter was written; sent on shore; and while Cromwell and Don Jorge discussed their wine, the Sara Jane was gliding over the bay, in the direction of the Narrows.[17]

The letter which Cromwell signed we shall see after a while.

PART VII. THE PEEP THROUGH
THE WALL OF THE PENITENTIARY.

Once more our narrative returns to the *supposed* father.

The next morning, between the hours of ten and eleven, a hackney coach deposited Mr. Hicks at the portal of the Eastern Penitentiary.

It was a bright and beautiful summer morning, and a clear blue sky smiled above the gloomy fabric, whose massive walls and sullen gate and ponderous towers present an imposing image of the feudal castle of the dark ages.

Situated on one of the most elevated sites in the county of Philadelphia—half way between Girard College and the Fairmount Basin—the Eastern Penitentiary is built of grayish granite, and covers about ten acres of ground. It stands almost alone, in the midst of desolate commons, with a Hospital near its front, the Dead House in its rear, and Potter's Field[18] not far away in the north-east. The corner-stone of this edifice was laid on the 22d of May, 1823: it was completed after nearly or quite ten years, at an expense which has never been clearly stated to the public. Perchance two millions of dollars were spent in its completion.

Within those gloomy walls, for years past, has been going on a solution of the question— "Is Solitary Confinement, attended with Labor, beneficial at once to the Commonwealth and the Criminal?"

We cannot say that the question has been satisfactorily answered in the affirmative.

For within the walls of this Bastile, and in years not very long ago—outrages have been committed upon Humanity which would have been a disgrace to the Bastile or the dungeons of the Inquisition in their worst days.

The difference between Hanging, as a punishment, and Solitary Confinement may be summed up in a few words:

To hang a man when you can punish his crime, and prevent his again violating the law, by other methods, is at best a cruel and cowardly punishment. Hanging is a quick, horrible and unnecessary death.

Hanging, however, bad as it is, and as much opposed as it is to the Law of Christ and Humanity, is only a murder of the Body.

Solitary Confinement is a murder of Body and Soul.

It is one of those punishments which man has no right to inflict upon man. It is the cruelty of the most barbarous age, sharpened and refined by the light and civilization of the nineteenth century. It is a slow death—a death of body and soul—a mouldering away of the soul within a withering body.

"Would you then," exclaims some friend of the system, which, often called Philanthropic, is truly and thoroughly Infernal— "Would you then do away at once with Hanging and with Solitary Confinement?"

Yes. By preventing instead of punishing crime. By spending the money which you now lavish upon gibbets, almshouses and jails, upon a broad system of education, which shall embrace all classes of society. By destroying those unjust laws which, by enriching one class continually tempt a portion of the other, and the largest class, to commit crime—crime sometimes committed to regain their own. But, in any case, and in the face of all emergencies, any punishment is better than Hanging or Solitary Confinement.

Mr. Jacob Hicks, properly and neatly dressed, with all the evidences of respectability about him, soon found entrance into the Penitentiary, where, presenting his permit, he asked to see "Elijah Watson, who has lately been convicted of a felony, and sentenced to some years in the Eastren[19] Penitentiary."

And in answer, Mr. Hicks was consigned to the care of an attendant, or under-keeper, who conducted him to the great central court yard, from which the various corridors of the Penitentiary diverge. They entered together one of those vast corridors which traverse the Bastile.

"Do wish merely to see the Prisoner, that is number Fifty-One?"

(When a man enters the Bastile he leaves his Name at the door. He becomes a Number.)

"That is all," answered Hicks in a low voice. "I only wish to peep at him."

The under-keeper opened a small aperture in the wall—used for the purpose of inspecting the prisoners—and through this aperture, Mr. Hicks gazed in silence, and beheld the prisoner.

It was a vaulted cell about twelve feet long, six feet wide, and the highest part of the ceiling was sixteen feet from the floor. Light was communicated by a large circular glass, fixed in the crown of the arch. This light fell upon the Prisoner. He was seated at a shoemaker's bench, engaged at making shoes, and his face upraised for a moment, received on every feature, the full glow of the light. It was the face of a boy of eighteen, hardened by hardship; the cheeks pale and sunken, the dark hair shaved closely around the forehead, and the eyes—leaden and lustreless—sunken deeply beneath the brows. There was a history in that face.

Clad in the prison garb, he was there alone, raising his dull eyes to the light, while his Father—the Rich Man, the Banker, the Merchant—gazed upon him, without the Convict being aware of his presence.

"He looks like my family," thought Mr. Jacob D. Z. Hicks, and made a sign to the under-keeper to close the aperture.

He then turned away, and with the attendant retraced his steps.

"What was he convicted for?" he asked.

"Passing counterfeit money. Didn't you see it in the papers? He passed a counterfeit note on the Tunkunny Bank; a ten dollar bill, I believe."

Now the Tunkunny Bank was one of Mr. Jacob Hick's banks, situated in an obscure country town; the greater part of the stock owned by himself; and although in good credit, Mr. Hicks knew that said Bank was in reality worth about ten cents in the dollar.

And for passing a counterfeit note on this Bank—in itself a counterfeit and cheat—his son was condemned to solitary confinement in the Eastern Penitentiary. Condemned that is, to be buried alive for the space of four years.

The Merchant made no answer to the attendant, but was silently conducted to the gate of the Bastile.

"How many years did you say?" he asked of the under-keeper,

as one foot beyond the portal, he stood between the outer world, and that Inner World, where Souls were rotting slowly away, in withering bodies.

"Four years," was the answer. "Judge Tomahawk sentenced him. He's supposed to be twenty-one, though I don't believe he's more than eighteen. He's been in a month."

Mr. Jacob D. Z. Hicks entered his carriage and drove away from the Penitentiary, leaving his son to his fate. He never saw him again until four years were over.

It was not until late in the afternoon that he went to his store.

Arrived at the counting room, he found Mr. Grimly in communication with the Broker, who had cashed the drafts presented by Cromwell the night before. It only required a few moments to put the Merchant in possession of the facts. And while Mr. Grimly was talking, a letter postmarked "New York" was put into the Merchant's hands. He read it and turned pale as ashes.

"It was all right, I 'spose," said the Broker, Mr. Whitely—"You told your son to get these drafts cashed?"

Mr. Hicks reflected a moment, while the tortures of a lost soul were at work within his breast. He hid his face in his bandanna, and wiped the perspiration from his brow.

"Five thousand and sixty dollars! At this time it will almost ruin me!" the thought flashed over him but did not escape his lips. "The dog! the scoundrel! He has his mother's blood in his veins, may the devil take him!"

"Did you say it was all right!" again remarked the Broker.

"Yes, yes—all right," replied the Merchant—"Those drafts were cashed at my orders."

—As soon as he was alone, relieved at once from Grimly and

the Broker, Mr. Hicks once more perused the letter "postmarked" New York, which had at first sight, excited such violent emotion.

DEAR FATHER:

You told me to follow my mother. I'm after her.

Yours affectionately,
CROMWELL HICKS.

P.S. That $5060 I have invested in the trade between *somewheres* and the Brazil coast. Refer to your friend Captain VELASQUEZ.

At the name "*Captain* VELASQUEZ,' the Merchant bit his nether lip.

"Where," he gasped, "Where did he learn that name?"

PART VIII. THE PRIVATE DEVOTIONS OF JACOB D. Z. HICKS.

There was a room in Mr. Hicks' mansion, which was never visited by any one, save himself. Located in an odd out-of-the-way corner of the huge pile of brick and mortar which constituted his town residence, this room was dedicated by Mr. Hicks to the thought and meditation of his most secret hours. Neither his wife, nor Cromwell, had ever passed its threshold. Mr. Hicks carried the key about him—in his pocket or next his heart—for what we know.

Was Mr. Hicks troubled in business? Straight he went up stairs and locked himself in his room—his room, by way of distinction, you understand. Had Mrs. Hicks been rather violent in her displays of bad temper? To his room hied Mr. Hicks without a moment's delay. Was Mr. Grimly in a "fluster" about some complicated matter of stocks, mortgages, notes of hand, or copper mines? No sooner had he opened his bosom to Mr. Hicks than Mr. Hicks went directly home, and locked himself up in his room. After three or four hours Mr. Grimly would receive his answer.

It was to this room that Mr. Hicks now hurried, with the letter of Cromwell in his hand. He entered the mansion without speaking to the servant—it was the heat of summer, and his usual list of servants had diminished to three, a cook, a waiter and a coachman—and passing through the splendidly furnished but silent chambers of his home, Mr. Hicks went up stairs, and did not once pause, until he stood before the narrow door of his room. It opened upon a stairway, and was sunken in the depths of a solid wall. Drawing forth the key, Mr. Hicks went in, and locked the door after him.

He was in darkness. But familiar in every nook and corner of the place, he soon discovered a box of Lucifer matches,[20] and by their aid lighted a half-burned spermaceti candle.

The light revealed a narrow room, with unpapered walls and uncarpeted floor. A small table and a chair was all that the place contained in the way of furniture. There was a single window, without sash or glass, but with a closed shutter, which was wood on the outside and iron within. Through small holes, pierced in the shutter, came the only breath of air which modified the stifling heat of the den. It was "fire proof;" the walls nearly four feet thick; and the door as well as the shutter lined with iron.

Mr. Hicks seated himself in the chair, placed the light and his hat upon the table, and spreading forth the letter of Cromwell, gazed at it earnestly and long, the perspiration streaming in bearded[21] drops from his forehead and cheeks.

"Velasquez!" he said—"how in the name of all that's infernal did he come by that name?"

The light shone over Mr. Hicks' face and form—both respectable in point of flesh—and showed his faultless broadcloth and cravat and vest as white as snow. There was nothing peculiar in Mr. Hicks' face; it was just such a visage as you see a thousand times a day, on Third street near Chesnut. The eyes were grey, the forehead bold, the cheeks slightly inclined to fullness, and the lips neither small nor large—lips which in their compression and in their unclosing said as plainly as lips can say, without speaking— "Three per cent a month is very good interest. I like it."

Understand, Mr. Hicks was no peculiar character; it was the object of his life to make money, and to keep up a fine appearance with the world; he was just as good a man as hundreds whom you meet every day, on Third street, or in the Exchange, or in any other Temple of Scrip and Stock; and was, withal, no better than any ninety-nine out of a hundred convicts in the Penitentiary. Out and out, through and through, Mr. Hicks was a business man—a perfect business man. Could we say more?

After pondering for a long time over the letter, in which the name of Captain VELASQUEZ was introduced, Mr. Hicks drew forth another key, and unlocked the door of a small iron safe, which stood beneath the table. It was an ugly rusted thing, looking something like one of those chests in which the Genii in the Arabian Nights are imprisoned; and had to all seeming seen many years of service. This chest was the Ark of the Covenant[22] in the eyes of Mr. Hicks—it contained the Covenant which he had made with the Devil—it contained his God.

He unlocked the safe, and drew forth the only thing it contained; a heavy volume, which resembled a merchant's Ledger, only it was bound in faded red morocco, and fastened with rusted iron clasps.

Mr. Hicks grasped the book eagerly, and undid the clasps, and stretched it forth upon the table, and gave himself to the enjoyment of its contents, like a gourmand to his feast.

In that book were entered all the "business operations" of Mr. Hicks for the last ten, yes, fifteen years. Not only those operations which were told to the world, under the head of the "stock market," but certain operations which Mr. Hicks and the Devil carried on for their especial benefit, having a perfectly good understanding with each other.

For instance, here was related in Mr. Hicks' own hand-writing, how he had procured the charters of three banks, situated in different parts of the country—owned and controlled by him—and not worth three cents on the dollar, although managed by our friend, they had in circulation at least $300,000 in bank notes.

Again: here was related how Mr. Hicks had bought a field in Jersey for $600, and called it a Copper Mine, and sold it, in $1000 shares, (to house-maids, hod-carriers, day-laborers, and such vulgar folk) at $25 per share. Mr. Hicks was, in fact, in his own person, the "Grand New Jersey and Gineywoyan Copper Mining Company."

Here, once more, were Mr. Hicks' little speculations in the way of Insurance Companies—Fire, Health, and Life Insurance

Companies—in all of which Mr. Hicks himself was the manager behind the scenes.

And here, in palpable red and black ink, were the transactions of Mr. Hicks and Captain Velasquez. These transactions had built up the fortune of Mr. Hicks. They were profitable, exceedingly profitable. They had been continued for a series of years, and had scarcely been interrupted by the seizure of a vessel now and then, and they had poured doubloons into Mr. Hicks' lap, in a sort of hail—a golden hail.

"And this scoundrel knows the name of Captain Velasquez!" said Mr. Hicks, after a long examination of the Book. "How has he gained his knowledge?"

Mr. Hicks saw danger looming from the horizon.

Leaning back in his chair, his eyes half closed, and the ends of his fingers placed together across his breast, Mr. Jacob D. Z. Hicks endeavored to arrange a plan for his future course.

After a long pause—the sweat streaming in hot drops from his brow—he thus delivered himself—

"These three Banks must break.[23] Copper stock, Life, Health, and Fire Insurance must follow their example. As for Mr. Jacob D. Z. Hicks, why heart-broken by the dissipation of his son, and the profligacy of his wife, he must suddenly *disappear*. A hat will be found on the wharf, and the world will lament the fall of the broken-hearted merchant, while Mr. Jacob D. Z. Hicks is safe in Havana.

He smiled one of his pleasant smiles—locked his own chest (having first put his God away) and then extinguished the candle.

"I can do nothing for that boy in the Penitentiary," he said, when the darkness enveloped him, "He must serve out his time."

Mr. Hicks left the room and locked it, and went on his way rejoicing.

But a month after this incident the three banks failed, Insurance Companies and Copper Mines went by the board, and the hat of Mr. Hicks (with an affecting letter in the lining) was found on the wharf. Who suffered by the failure of the Banks matters not; they were "poor devils" doubtless, that vulgar sort of folk who work for a living. It is their business to suffer.

Four years passed away. From 1845 to 1849 is a long step, but our Narrative leaves its various characters for four years, and it resumes their history in September, 1849, when the Killers appear upon the scene.

While four years pass, the Convict, Elijah Watson, makes shoes and *educates himself* in the Eastern Penitentiary.

And Cromwell, old Mr. Hicks and Don Jorge—where are they? Where are they?

PART IX. THE SILENT COMPOSITOR.

In the latter part of September, 1849, a pale faced man, dressed in shabby black, came to a printing office in the city of Philadelphia, and obtained employment as a Compositor. It was one of those printing offices which, from garret to cellar, abound with the evidences of life, bustle, and business. From the power-presses underground, to the Compositor's room in the sky, this establishment was devoted to setting type, printing books, papers and handbills, folding, stitching, binding—and we're not sure—but stereotyping in the bargain. You could hand in your MSS.[24] at one door, and get your book, bound and lettered, at another.

Whether this huge building was situated up an alley, or on a public street, is a question which, at the present moment, does not need an answer.

Let us enter the Compositor's room on the fourth story. The rain beats with a gloomy patter against its many windows. It is a long room, narrow in proportion to its width, with "cases" stationed near each window. In front of each case (there were eight or ten in all) stands a compositor, working in silence at his task; and in the centre of the room, near a huge slab of black marble elevated on a table, you behold the foreman, who is engaged in making up the form.

The pale compositor in the shabby dress is at his case in one corner, the light from the window falling over his projecting forehead. He does his work—goes to his meals—returns again—and in the same quiet unobtrusive manner.

Now among the compositors in this office there is at least one boy compositor to every man. The boys are employed to do men's work, in a bungling manner, at half wages. The men, thus thrown out of employ, may get drunk or steal, but that is no business of the Proprietor. He, good man, is employed in printing tracts, books, and newspapers—and among his greatest patrons are certain benevolent societies, who *give away* tracts and books, and print newspapers at $1.00 per year. Thus liberal, these societies must have their printing done at half price. The Proprietor cannot afford to pay full wages; he employs one half boys, and makes up the rest by cutting down the wages of the girls in the bindery. Thus he is enabled to print "The Gospel Christian" (a weekly paper) together with omnibus loads of tracts and books, at something lower than half price. So glorious a thing is a Benevolent or Religious (!) Society, which *gives* away the life and bread of book-binder girls and printers.

Now on the day on which we behold these compositors, men and boys, at their work, (while the Foreman, Mr. Snick, a wiry little man, with the reminiscences of a black whisker under his chin, is making up the form of "The Gospel Christian") an event, rather important to the comprehension of our Narrative, is fast maturing towards completion.

The hour of twelve arrives; the pale compositor takes his hat and coat, and goes to his dinner. The Foreman disappears into the lower story. But the other compositors, men and boys, gathered around the "imposing stone," (as the black marble slab is styled) mingle in rapid conversation, and hold what may be termed a Council of War.

"You don't say so?" whispers a tall compositor—"By Jove! I thought something of that kind was the matter!"

"I never liked his looks—" adds one of the boys—a very promising youth, who takes a pugilistic entertainment with one of the other boys, whenever the Foreman turns his back.

"Nor I—he has a downcast look!" adds another:

"His eyes are too deep set!"

"He never speaks to any one, in a voice above his breath."

While the compositors—boys and men—thus deliver their opinions, there is one who does not speak until all the others have concluded. He is a thin, slender personage—grown pale from working late at night on a daily paper—and with dull eyes, that seem to have had all their life boiled out of them, over a slow fire.

"Why don't you speak, Corny?" asks one of the boys—"Why don't you give your opinion about the *new* compositor?"

Conscious that he has an important secret in his possession, Mr. Corny Walput folds his arms, and looks at his companions with a wink of his boiled eyes, and a twist of his colorless lips.

"What's the name of the *new* compositor?" he asks.

"Trottle—Job Trottle," responds one of the boys.

"Where did he come from?" continued Mr. Walput.

"From Washington. He says he's been employed in the Union office," was the answer.

Mr. Corny Walput put his thumb to his nose.

"Gammon!" he ejaculated. "His name aint Job Trottle, and he didn't come from Washington."

"Who is he?" the compositors cried in a breath.

But Mr. Corny Walput was mysterious. Winking and twisting his mouth, he bade his companions "Wait until the Foreman comes—wait until Snick comes. *Then* I'll show you fireworks."

They did wait until the foreman came. But while they discussed their dinners (and most of them brought their dinners with them) they did not forget to also discuss the pale-faced compositor in the shabby black coat.

At length, about one o'clock, "Mr. Job Trottle" returned, and took his place quietly at his case, amid the winks, nods and whispers of the other compositors. The pugilistic youth was particularly happy in making ugly faces; nature had done a great deal for him, but he assisted nature.

Next entered Mr. Snick. Complacent with a good dinner, and twirling that bit of whisker, under his chin, Mr. Snick resumed his place at the imposing stone. Corny approached—they exchanged whispers—Snick opened his eyes, and Corny pointed to the silent compositor. Then Snick grew red in the face, and pale again, whispering "My goodness!" three times, in a voice of evident horror. Corny resumed his whispers, and then Snick hurried down stairs, and had a little private talk with the Proprietor. When Snick came back, his face was glowing with excitement; he stepped over the floor with the consciousness that all eyes were fixed upon him. He twirled that fragmentary whisker with almost a savage air. The compositors, boys and men, ceased their labors—all save the silent one, who, with downcast head, worked away in his corner.

"Eh—ah—ehem!" and Snick tapped the silent compositor on the shoulder—"Mr. Trottle! I think you said your name was Trottle?"

The silent compositor had been setting upon an article for the "Gospel Christian," entitled "The Gospel nature of the Gallows." He turned, as Mr. Snick spoke, and looked at him, like a man who has been disturbed in the midst of a reverie. His projecting brow, pale cheeks, and eyes deep sunken, were half in light and half in shadow.

"What did you say, Sir?" he said in a low voice, and with the manner of an absent man.

"I *think* that you said your name was Job Trottle?" said Mr. Snick, very slowly.

"I did, and so it is," and the silent compositor turned to his task again.

Mr. Snick seemed for a moment confounded by the quiet manner of the individual. Gathering courage, (and with Corny at his back, attended by one boy and two men) he again tapped "Mr. Job Trottle" on the arm

"No, Sir," he said, in a voice between a bluster and a whine—
"No, Sir. Your name aint Job Trottle, but it is Elijah Watson. Do
you hear that, Sir, Elijah Watson?"

The silent compositor started, as though a sharp pain had
smote him in the heart. His face grew red as blood. He surveyed
Mr. Snick, while his eyes seemed at once to sink deeper in their
sockets, and flash up with a sinister glare.

"Yes," continued Snick, gathering courage from the compositors, who, man and boy, had ranged themselves at his back (the
pugilistic youth making frightful faces all the while;) "Yes, your
name is Elijah Watson, and you haven't come from Washington,
but you have come from the Eastern Penitentiary, where you've
been spendin' four years for passing counterfeit money. Now, what
do you think of your brass, to come and pass yourself off as an
honest man? In this here office, too, where nothing but moral,
well-behaved people are tolerated—why —"

Snick paused for breath, and the silent compositor stood with
one arm resting on his case, while he took a hurried glance at the
group before him. His face flushed, and was pale again; there was
a straining at the muscles of his throat, and then he turned his face
toward the window. What was passing in his heart God only knows.

Snick, taking this for a sign of cowardice, resumed his elegant
strain—

"To come here, in the office of the Gospel Christian (not men-
tioning any quantity of tracts and books which are published under
this roof) and pass yourself off as an honest man! Why, I never
heard of—"

"How did type settin' go out yonder?" interrupted the pugilistic youth.

"Rayther confinin'—aint it?" remarked Corny—"has a depressin' influence on the sperrits, I'm told?"

The convict turned, and cast his eye toward the nail where his coat was hanging. He was deathly pale; the muscles of his face were knit; he shook from head to foot.

"Let me pass you, if you please," he said in a very low voice—the tone of a man who is endeavoring to choke down some violent burst of passion.

Mr. Snick didn't like the expression of his deep sunken eye, so he let him pass. And the compositors gave way, Corny slinking in the background, while the pugilistic youth, in the extreme van, kept up his pantomime of frightful faces.

The convict did not speak, but turning his back upon them all, walked quietly across the floor, and put on his coat, and drew his cap over his brows. Then, still keeping his face toward the wall, he walked across the floor and descended the stairway, drawing his cap deeply over his brows, as he disappeared from view.

This silence—this struggling of the poor wretch with his emotion—this exit made without a word, and without even asking for the money which was due him—was not without its effect upon foreman and compositors.

"Come back," cried Snick, running to the head of the stairs— "I owe you two dollars and a half—"

But the convict was gone beyond the reach of his voice. One of the compositors, not quite so *virtuous* as the rest (though he had tacitly assented to the moral of this scene) whispered to Snick— received two dollars and a half in silver—and, without hat or coat, rapidly descended the stairway. He passed through press-room, bindery and ware-room, in his eager search after the convict; and his search being fruitless, he descended the long dark stairway which led to the street.

Up and down the street he looked, and to the right and left, but the convict had disappeared.

"Well," ejaculated the compositor, as he stood clinking the half dollars in his hands—"The face of that fellow has left quite an impression on me. I think it would been just as well if Corny had kept his tongue, and Snick had minded his own business."

And so it would.

We shall see the "silent compositor" again.

PART X. THE SUPERNUMERARY.

In the month of October, 1849, a young woman, who was connected with one of the theatres in a subordinate capacity, excited considerable attention on the part of those gentlemen who prowl about the stage, seeking "whom they may devour." We allude to that class of characters, young and old, who insult respectable women in the street, parade opera glasses in the pit, while the dancing is in progress, and hang around the green room, where the actors congregate when their presence is not needed upon the stage.

This young woman was altogether a subordinate; she did not appear in any leading character, but was seen as an assistant in the ballet, or as a part of some dramatic spectacle; in fact she was what is generally denominated a "supernumerary." She was about eighteen years of age; rather tall; with brown hair, dark eyes, a noble bust, and a walk that would not have disgraced an empress. She was new to the stage. Who or what she was, no one knew; not even the manager who paid her thirty-seven and a half cents per night for her services in the *ballet* and spectacle. She had only been engaged a week, in October, 1849, when her beauty made a considerable buz among the libertines of the pit, and the loungers of the green room. Her modest manner, and her evident desire to remain unobserved and unknown, only whetted the curiosity of these vultures, who prey upon female innocence and beauty.

One night, however, as winding her faded shawl about her shoulders, and drawing her green veil over her face, she left the theatre, on her way to her unknown home, she was followed—at a discreet distance—by one of those gentlemen of the character named above. He was rather portly; wore a bangup[25] which concealed the lower part of his face, and carried a large bone-headed stick. The object of his pursuit led him a devious chase. Up one street and down another, now passing through narrow alleys, and now along the streets, she hurried on, until at last she reached a small frame house, which stood at the extremity of a dark court, in that district somewhat widely known as "Moyamensing." This court is known in the language of the District by the euphonious name of "Dog Alley." A lamp standing at the entrance of the Court emitted a faint and dismal light. When she reached the lamp she paused, and looked around her, as though she was conscious or afraid that she had been followed. The gentleman with the big stick saw her turn, and skulked behind a convenient corner, in time to avoid her observation. In a moment she resumed her way and entered the frame tenement, from the window of which a faint light shone out upon the pavement.

The portly gentleman stole cautiously to the window, took one glance, and then crouched against the door of the house. That glance, however, had revealed to him a small room miserably furnished, with an old woman sitting near a smouldering fire, and a young one—the "supernumerary" of the theatre—standing by her side, one hand laid upon a pine table, and the other raised as if in the act of expostulation.

The portly gentleman did his best to overhear the conversation which took place between the two. Pressing his ear against the chink of the door, and balancing himself with his stick, as he kneeled on one knee, he managed to hear a portion of their conversation.

"So you've come—have you?" said the old woman, in a voice between a grunt and a growl.

"Yes, mother. And there's my week's salary—just three dollars."

"Three dollars! And how's a body as is old and has the rheumatiz to live on three dollars?"

"Mother I do all that I can, I'm sure. I'd earn more if I could."

"Bah! If you only know'd what's what you might earn a heap, I tell you. Here since your father's been dead—killed by fallin' off a buildin' four years ago—I've had all the keer of you and tuk in washin' when you was goin' to school. Yes, I tuk you from the Factory and sent you to school. And now when you've grow'd up and kin do somethin' for your mother, why don't you do it?"

"What *can* I do, mother?" said the young woman, in a voice of entreaty.

The old woman replied with a sound between a cough and a laugh, as she said:

"What kin you do? Why if I was young and handsom' and had a foot and a face like yourn—and danced at the thea*ter*, I'd show you, what *I* could do. Aint there plenty of rich gentlemen, as 'ud be glad to pay you your weight in goold if—

The rest of the sentence was lost in a whisper, but the gentleman in the big stick, who listened at the door, heard the reply of the girl, which consisted in a simple ejaculation, uttered in a tone of reproach and shame—

"My God, Mother!"

"Yes, it is easy to say My God, Mother!" replied the old woman mimicking her daughter, "But if you only had the spunk of a lobster you might roll in goold an' be a great actress and—what not!"

The listener did not wait for another word, but pushing open the door, entered the apartment. The old woman looked up in surprise, her haggard face looking almost ghastly, by lamplight, while the daughter (who had thrown her bonnet and shawl aside) gazed upon the intruder in evident alarm.

"Don't mind me, my good friends, don't mind me," said the portly gentleman, in a thick voice, as he approached the table. "I'm a friend, that's all. Have seen your daughter on the stage, and would like to make a great actress of her. Am a theatrical manager—just over the water—in search of American talent. Will take charge of her tuition. That can't be managed without money, but money's no object to me."

And stepping between the mother and daughter he laid five bright gold pieces upon the pine table.

"Here's luck!" screeched the old woman, grasping for the money.

"What say you?" asked the portly gentleman, addressing the daughter.

"I—don't—know—you—sir—" she exclaimed with a proud curl of the lip, as her bosom swelled under its shabby covering. At the same time she wrenched the money from her mother's grasp. "Take your money Sir."

There was something queenly in the look of the young woman, as, with her form swelling to its full stature, she regarded the intruder with a look of withering scorn, extending his gold pieces in one hand and at the same time pointing to the door.

"The very thing! That voice would do honor to Fanny Kemble![26] I tell you, Miss, that nature cut you out for an actress—a great actress."

"So natur' did," exclaimed the old woman, rising from the chair—"Take the money, gal, and let this gentleman make a great actress of you."

"Either you must leave this house, or I will," said the girl, and dashing the gold pieces into the face of the portly gentleman, she retreated behind the table, her eye flashing and her bosom swelling with anger. This action rather disconcerted the gentleman. Retreating backward, and bowing at the same time, he stumbled over the threshold, and gathered himself up in time to receive the gold pieces from the hand of the girl. She had gathered them from the floor in defiance of the objurgations of her mother, who earnestly sought to retain only a single piece.

"Now, mother," said the girl, closing the door and placing her hand firmly on the old woman's shoulder, "If after this I hear one word from your lips, like those you have spoken to-night, we part forever."

Her flashing eye and deep toned voice impressed the old woman with a sensation between rage and fear. But ere she could frame a reply, her daughter had gone up stairs, and the old woman heard a sound like the closing of a bolt.

"One of her tantrums. When things don't go right, she goes to bed without supper, and locks herself in. Lor' how they brings up children now-a-days!"

For a long time she sat in silence, stretching her withered hands over the fire: at length she took the light, and hobbling to the door, unlocked it, and went out into the court. Bending down, the light extended in her skinny fingers and playing over her haggard face, she groped in the mud and filth for the gold pieces which her daughter had flung in the face of the portly gentleman.

"Won," she mumbled, seizing a bright object which sparkled in the mud, when a hand touched her lightly on the arm, and looking up she saw the portly gentleman at her side.

He pointed to the door of the frame house, and led the way. She followed, and after closing the street door and the door which opened on the stairway, they sat down together and conversed for a long time in whispers, the old woman's face manifesting a feverish lust for gain, while the portly gentleman removed his hat and suffered his coat collar to fall on his shoulders, until his face was visible.

It was the face of a very pleasant looking gentleman, whose forehead was relieved by masses of curling black hair, and beneath whose ample chin appeared a half circle of whiskers—glossy whiskers, well oiled and curled, and shown in contrast with a white shirt bosom, which sparkled with a diamond pin. This gentleman, without the hair and whiskers, would have been at least fifty-four years old—but with hair and whiskers (both were false) he looked only forty-two.

There was a bright twinkle in his eye, half hidden in wrinkled lids, and a sort of amorous grin upon his lips. He approached the old woman and talked in a low oily voice.

They conversed for a long time and the end of the conversation was in these words:—

"To-morrow night, as she is going to the theatre," said the gentleman.

"It is election night[27] and the streets will be full of bonfires and devilment. She can be seized at the corner of the street, put in a cab which I have ready, and kept quiet until her temper is a little managable."

He laid some bank notes and bright gold pieces upon the table, which the old woman seized with a hungry grasp, as she replied:

"Yes, and Black Andy is the man to do it. Have everything ready and it kin be done. You'd better see Andy; he keeps a groggery at the corner of the court."

"The Gentleman" rose, and bidding the dame good night, proceeded to the "Hotel" of a huge negro, who went by the name of Black Andy, or the "Bulgine,"[28] in the more familiar dialect of Moyamensing. Picking his way through the darkness, he presently entered a low and narrow room, filled with stench and smoke, with negroes—men, women, and children huddled together in one corner, and a bar in the other, behind which stood the negro himself, dealing out whiskey to a customer. The scene was lighted by three tallow candles, stuck in as many porter bottles. The "Bulgine" was a huge, burly negro, black as the ace of spades, with a mouth like a gash, a nose that looked as if it had been trodden upon, and fists that might have felled an ox. The customer was a white man—rather tall and muscular—dressed in a miserable suit of grey rags, with his hair worn long before the ears, and a greasy cloth cap drawn low over his forehead.

"This 'ere whiskey burns like rale—," grunted the customer, concluding his sentence with a blasphemous expression.

"Dat it does. It am de rale stripe—hot as pepper an' brimstone."

After these words, "the Loafer" in grey rags stretched himself on the floor, and our worthy gentleman approached the negro.

A few words sufficed to put the negro in possession of the object of the gentleman's visit. He grinned horribly, as the worthy man bent over the counter, and communicated his desire in a confiding whisper.

"Dars my hand on it," he said, "For a small matter o' fifty dollars dis Bulgine put twenty gals in a cab."

"To-morrow night—remember. The old lady's agreeable and I'll have the cab at the street corner. There's twenty-five on account."

"Y-a-s sah, dat's de talk," responded the negro grasping the money.

"Who's that fellow?" whispered the Gentleman, touching with his foot the prostrate form of the the[29] "Loafer," who by this time was snoring lustily.

"Dat—eh, dat? I raly dono his name—but he's a Killer."

PART XI. THE KILLERS.

This seemed perfectly satisfactory to the Gentleman, who drew his hat over his brows, pulled up the collar of his coat and leaving the groggery, made the best of his way homeward.

After his visiter[30] had gone, the Bulgine approached the prostrate loafer, and kicked him with his splay foot.

"Get out o' dis. Dis 'ain't no place for you, dam white trash."

The loafer arose grumbling, and lounged lazily to the door, which the Black Bulgine closed after him, with the objurgation— "De dam Killer; dar room is better as dar company."

No sooner, however, had the Loafer passed from the groggery into the court, than his lazy walk changed into a brisk stride, his head rose on his shoulders, and he seemed to have become in a moment altogether a new man.

He passed from the court into the street, where a couple of ruffian-like men stood beneath the light of the street lamp. As he approached them, he made a sign with his right hand, and the two ruffians followed him like dogs obeying the whistle of a master. Along the dark and deserted street the loafer pursued his way, until he came to the corner of a well-known street leading from the Delaware to the Schuylkill; a street which, by the bye, was lighted at every five yards by a groggery or a beer shop. At the corner, and near the door of every groggery, stood groups of men, or half-grown boys—sometimes five and sometimes six or seven in a group. The Loafer passed them all, repeating the sign which he had given to the first two ruffians. And at the sign the men and half-grown boys fell in his wake; by the time he had gone half a square, he was followed by at least twenty persons, who tracked his footsteps without a word. For a quarter of an hour they walked on, the silence only broken by the shuffling of their feet. At length arriving before an unfinished three-story brick house (unfinished on account of the numerous riots which have so long kept the District of Moyamensing in a panic) they silently ranged themselves around the "Loafer," whose sign they had followed.

"All Killers?" he said, anxiously scanning the visages of the ruffians, boys and men, who were only dimly perceptible by the star-light.

"All Killers," was the answer.

The "LOAFER" again made a sign with his right hand, which

was answered by the others, and then exclaimed—"Come boys—we've work to do. Let us enter the Den of the Killers."

And one by one they descended into the cellar of the unfinished house—the "Loafer" being the last. Indeed he remained on the verge of the cellar door, for a few moments after the others had disappeared. He looked anxiously up and down the street, and placing two fingers in his mouth, emitted a long and piercing whistle. It was answered in a moment, and from behind the corner of the building came a person, whose slim form was muffled in the thick folds of a cloak.

"All right?" said the new comer—and his cloak falling aside for a moment, disclosed the glare of a uniform.

"All right," answered the "Loafer"—"The boys are ripe for fun. Let us go up after them.—What! You're not afraid?" he continued as the other displayed some signs of hesitation.

"Not afraid Dick, but—you're sure of them?" whispered the man in the cloak.

"I wish I was as sure of a safe landing in Cuba, one month hence. Come along, my boy! "The Killers and Cuba!" that's the word. Come, and let me show you the Den of the Killers!"

He grasped the hand of the stranger and they descended into the cellar.

PART XII. A YOUNG MAN WHO DESIRES TO KNOW "THE NAME OF HIS FATHER."

Before we follow "the Loafer" and his uniformed friend into "the Den of the Killers," we will return to the house of the old woman, in the classic retreat of "Dog Alley." No sooner had "the gentleman" left her than she was surprised by the entrance of a new visitor. This is the way it happened.

The old woman was once more alone, sitting beside the pine table, crumpling the notes between her fingers, while her lips moved in a half coherent soliloquy:

"Seems to me I've seen his face afore. I'll bet punkins on it. If it wasn't for the whiskers and the hair, I'd think—"

"Good evening, Mother," said a voice at her shoulder—"How d'ye get along, anyhow?"

The speaker (who had entered unperceived while she was wrapt in her brown study) was a young man of not more than twenty-three years, in fact, although he looked nearly five years older. Dressed in a shabby black coat, buttoned to the neck, with an old cloth cap drawn over his forehead, he stood near the pine table, his right hand grasping a knotted stick. His voice was singularly hollow and husky in its every accent. The lamplight revealed his sunken cheeks, and deep-set eyes, as he stood there regarding the old woman with a half mocking grin.

"Oh, it's you, is it? said the old woman with a start—"A purty time o' night for you to show yourself! This blessed two weeks I haven't clapped eyes on you—and for that matter, upon a penny o' your money nayther."

"How should I get money, Mother?" said the young man, in a quiet tone, but as he spoke the grin widened over his colorless features.

"Work!" and the old woman clutched her gold and notes, and put her hands under her shawl.

"Work!" he echoed—"Didn't I try? First at the printin' office, among printers, and you know what *they* did—don't you? Then as a porter at a shoemaker's shop, among shoemakers, and you know what *they* did—don't you? Then as a porter in a store, among porters and draymen, and you know what *they* did—don't you? Can you tell me what name I went by at all these places?"

He bent down, and drew closer to the old woman, his eyes flashing, while he shook with suppressed laughter.

"Did I go by the name of Job Trottle, or by the name of Elijah Watson, Convict 'Number Fifty-One,' in the Eastern Penitentiary?"

"Kin I help it?" said the old woman, almost savagely—"Kin I help it ef you don't get work a-cause you was in the State's Prison?"

Elijah did not at once reply. Throwing his cap upon the table, he disclosed his protuberant forehead, encircled by his dark hair, closely cut. He came a step nearer Mrs. Watson (for the reader doubtless recognizes our old friend of Runnel's Court,) and folding his arms, looked at her steadily, as he said in a low voice—

"I don't say you can help it, but I'll tell you what you can help. You can help keepin' me in the dark about things I want to know, and things that I must know."

"What things?"

"Don't sham stupid, old woman, for it won't help you now. I want to know the name of a certain gentleman, who came to see you after I'd been a month in the Penitentiary, and who you suspected was nobody else but my father. Don't you remember you told me so, when you came to see me at Cherry Hill, soon afterwards? Yes, you told me what a nice man he was—such a pleasant white cravat as he wore—and how you followed him from Runnel's Court, and found out who he was. And how, when you'd found out his name, you hunted up a certain old letter from my mother, and found out that this identical gentleman was my father, and nothin' else. You didn't tell him that you had a letter from my mother, or that you knew her name—you kept that *dark* with me. Now, do you hear me? Here I stand. and there you are, and you've got to tell me that old gentleman's name, or I'll know the reason why!"

While Elijah was speaking, Mrs. Watson looked up, at first in wonder, and then with a sort of mingled fear and amazement. For violent passions were struggling upon the colorless features of the Convict; his lips fairly writhed as he spoke; and the veins stood out, swollen and purpled, upon his projecting brow.

"Lije, don't make a fool of yesself. Sit down, and cool yer dander. What's the good o' yer knowing the man's name?"

Elijah brought his stick upon the table, with a sound like the report of a pistol.

"That name, I say!" he shouted, in a voice that was thick and husky with struggling passions. "That name, afore you speak another word, or by — I'll go to Cherry Hill for somethin' worse than passin' counterfeit money. Now, perhaps you understand me?"

"Lije, it won't do you no good; he's dead," cried Mrs. Watson, who trembled with fright.

At these words the Convict fell back a step, while his face displaye the very distortion of mental torture in every writhing outline.

"Dead! You aint lyin'?" he ejaculated.

"He was drowned only a little while arter he came to see me in Runnel's Court. It won't do you no good to know his name. As for your mother, she died in Montreal last year. When she heard of the old man's death, she sent me some money, and the next I heer'd was that she was dead."

"And so you won't tell me the name of my father?" said Elijah, bending across the table, until his face nearly touched the old woman's shoulder.

"It won't do you no good, fur—"

He reached forth his brawny hand, and clutched her by the throat—"Now," he whispered, as, half suffocated, she endeavored to tear his grip from her throat—"Now, tell me his name, or I'll choke you dead."

Gasping for breath, the old woman managed to murmur, "Take your hand from my throat, and I'll tell." Elijah at once released his grasp. "No foolin,' old woman, you must tell me the name an' take your Bible oath upon it."

"His name," answered the old woman, "was John Tomson, and—"

"Will you swear to *that?*" fiercely interrupted the Convict. "Now, I know his name wasn't John Tomson, for about three months arter I was in jail, the underkeeper told me of a gentleman who came and peeped at me through a hole in the wall. This gentleman was exactly like the one who visited you in Runnel's Court- I know his name, and I jist want to see if you have truth enough in you to tell it to me. What was the name of my father? By the long days and nights I spent at Cherry Hill, I *wont* ask you that question again."

The old woman was now thoroughly frightened. It was her first impulse to raise the cry of murder, but when she looked at the face of the Convict—ferocious with a strange determination—she abandoned this idea.

"The name o' the old gentleman, who came to see me in Runnel's Court, was Hicks—Jacob D. Z. Hicks—and he was drowned about three months arterward. He was very rich, or folks said that he was, but his creditors arter he was dead had to whistle for their money. An' he's the man I tuk to be your father—s' 'elp me God!"

Long before she had concluded, the savage look of the Convict had been replaced by an expression of blank despair.

"Jacob D. Z. Hicks!" the words came from his lips in an under tone—"That's the the[31] name. That's the man who looked at me through the hole in the wall. And he's dead, yes—" his voice rose into a shriek, as he clutched his stick with both hands—"He's *where* I can't get at him."

Apparently overwhelmed by the violence of his emotions, he sank into a chair, and buried his face in his hands. The old woman could hear him murmur, in tones that were alternately deep with rage, or tremulous with almost unmanly feeling—

"That's the name. That's it. And he looked at me through the hole in the jail, and did not stir a hand for me. And he knew that I had been put in, for passing a counterfeit note on his own bank—and knew that I was his son. He did. And now when I come out o' jail, the word "Convict" follers me everywhere, and shuts me out from every hope of ever gettin' an honest livelihood—yes, Langfeldt,[32] who was hung last fall, was better off than I am! I think I'd go ten years in the Penitentiary jist for the chance o' havin' five minutes talk with this father of mine!"

"What 'ud you do with him, Lije?"

"Talk with him"—he raised his face; there were tears in his fiery eyes—"Talk with him, that's all."

For a little while they sat in silence; the old woman "huddled up" in her shawl, and Elijah with his face buried in his hands. At length he rose, put on his cap, and approached the pine table—

"Where's Kate?" he said—"I have not seen her these two weeks."

"Up stairs—asleep," was the answer.

"Now look here, I'm a goin' to do somethin' that will set me up for life, or—*never mind what.* I know your disposition, and know you'd make no more bones of sellin' Kate to the devil, than you would of eatin' your breakfast. If I succeed in what I'm goin' to undertake, Kate will hear from me. Tell her that, and she will receive from me, what will put her out of want for life. For though she aint my sister by blood, she is my sister in fact; we've been brought up together, and I think more of her than a dozen sisters by blood. If I fail, old woman, why you'll never hear of me again. In that case I'll be a dead man, or a 'Number' in some jail or other. But don't you put any of your devil's tricks to work about Kate—if you ever bring harm to her, by the living —, I'll come back and haunt you, though I'm dead as dead can be. Good night, old woman."

He moved to the door—

"Where are you goin', Lije?"

"To complete my *education*," he said, turning his head over his shoulder, with a broad grin upon his colorless face—"You see, when I was out at Cherry Hill, they brought me a Bible, and set me to readin' and thinkin'—they did. They spoke sich smooth words to me, while they were buryin' me alive in that stone coffin. They did. And now I'm goin' to complete the education which they begun. Good night, old woman."

With these words he left the hovel, and as the door closed on him, the old woman, still "crumpling" the bank notes in her fingers, muttered to herself—

"Where have I seen that gentleman afore? I think I know him spite of his black hair and whiskers?"

She did not allude to Elijah, but to the gentleman with whom she had contracted the ruin of poor Kate. She sat there alone, until the lamp flickered its last, and then crawled up stairs to the miserable bed, first stopping a moment to listen at the door of her daughter's room. All was quiet there. Poor Kate, whom she had deliberately sold to the "English Manager," otherwise known as the "Gentleman," was sleeping the sound sleep of innocence and toil.

PART XIII. THE DEN OF THE KILLERS.

Now we return to the Loafer and his friend in uniform, whom we left for a short time in part XI.

The Loafer jumped into the cellar of the unfinished house, and was followed by his friend, whose slim figure and bright uniform was hidden in his cloak. Scrambling in silence through the dark cellar, they ascended in the darkness into the upper rooms of the unfinished house, the Loafer leading his friend by the hand. Arriving at the head of the second flight of stairs, where a faint light came through a window, the Loafer said:

"Wait here a minute, Captain. I'll go in and see the boys. Do you hear 'em?"

"Hear them?" said the Captain, with something of a foreign accent—"Do you think I'm deaf?"

He did indeed hear them, for a clamor like Babel resounded from a room which was divided from the entry on the third floor by a partition of lath and plaster. Shrouding himself in his cloak, the Captain leaned against the wall, and looked out of the window, while the Loafer entered the room from which the clamor proceeded.

It was somewhat gorgeously lighted—the candles being of tallow, and porter bottles serving for candlesticks. The walls, although but newly plastered, were black with smoke, and ornamented with the heraldic devices of the Killers, such as

"THE KILLERS FOR EVER!"

Or again, in a more lively vein,

"GO IT KILLERS!"

Or yet once more

"DOWN WITH THE BOUNCERS!"

(The Bouncers, be it understood, are a rival gang of desperadoes.) The room was destitute of chairs or tables; indeed it was without furniture of any kind. The porter bottles containing the candles were arranged at various distances from each other—in a sort of an oblong circle—along the uncarpeted floor.

Around each candle, seated on the floor, was a group of men and boys, who were drinking bad whiskey—fingering dirty cards—smoking pestilential segars—and swearing vigorously in the intervals of whiskey, cards, and cigars. These were the Killers, and this was the Den of the Killers.

And into this foul den entered the Loafer in his grey rags. He was hailed by a "Hurrah for Bob Blazes, the Captain of the Killers!" He answered the shout in as hearty a manner, and then flinging a couple of dollars on the floor, added, "Some more rum, boys! We may as well make a night of it."

Then looking beneath the front of his cap, he silently surveyed "the Killers." It was a fine spectacle. They were divided into three classes—beardless apprentice boys who, after a hard day's work, had been turned loose upon the street, at night, by their Masters or "Bosses"—young men of nineteen and twenty who, fond of excitement, had assumed their name and joined the gang for the mere fun of the thing, and who would either fight for a man or knock him down, just to keep their hand in—and fellows with countenances that reminded you of a brute and devil, well intermingled. These last were the smallest in the number, but the most ferocious of the three. These, the third class, not more than ten in number, were the very worst specimens of the savage of this large city. Brawny fellows, with faces embruted by hardship, rum, and crime, they were "just the boys" to sack a theatre or burn a church.

It was to these that Bob Blazes, the Leader of the Killers, addressed himself.

"Come, lieutenants, let's go into the next room. While the boys have their fun here, we'll cut out some fun for to-morrow. To-morrow's 'lection day."

The eleven ruffians rose at his bidding, and followed him into the next room, the foremost carrying a porter bottle in his hand.

This room was larger than the first, and along the windows which opened upon the street, rough pieces of pine board were nailed. Rougher pieces of old carpet were huddled in the corners— these were the beds of the "lieutenants" in which they slept away the day, after a night of rum and riot—and the mantelpiece was adorned with broken pipes and empty bottles. The walls were quite pictorial, being plastered over with theatre bills, on which the names of "Jakey," "Mose," and "Lize" appeared in conspicuous letters; thus hinting at the fact in city life, that the pit of the theatre sometimes educates Killers, even as the box of the theatre very often produces full fledged puppies, who carry hair on their upper lips and opera-glasses in their hands.

Taking his position in the centre of the room, with the eleven ruffians around him, Bob Blazes surveyed their hang-dog faces in silence for a few moments, and then began:

"In a week, my boys, we'll start for Cuba. 'Cuba, gold, and Spanish women,' that's our motto! You know that I'm in communication with some of the heads of the Expedition; I was told to pick out the most desperate devils I could find in Moyamensin'. I've done so. You've signed your names, and received your first month's pay. In a week you'll go on to New York with me, and then hurrah for 'Cuba, gold, and Spanish women!'"

"Hurrah for 'Cuba, gold, and Spanish women!'"

Bob Blazes raised his cap, and displayed a sunburnt face, encircled by sandy whiskers, and with the scar of a frightful wound under the left eye. There was a kind of ferocious beauty about that countenance. It was the face of a man of twenty-three, who has seen and suffered much, and known life on land and sea, in brothel and bar-room, and, perhaps, in the — Jail.

"Wait a minute, boys, and I'll show you something," said Bob, and, without another word, hurried from the room. In a moment he returned, holding a cloaked figure by the hand, much to the surprise and wonder of the Killers.

"This is your Captain. Captain JACK JONES, allow me to make you acquainted with the very cream of the Killers. Three cheers, my boys, for Jack Jones!"

And while the cheers shook the room, the stranger removed his hat—disclosing a dark complexioned and whiskered face—and flung his cloak upon his right arm—thus revealing a very handsome blue and gold uniform, which fitted his slender form, like a glove to a woman's hand. Jack Jones bowed and laid his hand upon his heart, and said, in good English, spiced with a Spanish accent—

"Gentlemen, I'm exceedingly proud to meet you." As he said this, his dark eyes twinkled under the dark brows, and he gave a twist to his jet black mustache. "I have a trifle here, in the way of coin, which I'd like to see expended on our outfit—" He scattered some gold pieces on the floor with the air of a theatrical King giving away theatrical money— "And our friend, Bob Blazes, here, will explain the rest."

With these words he resumed his hat and cloak and stepped to the door, while the Killers—all save one—were scrambling for the money. When they had accomplished this feat, they looked around for Captain Jack Jones, but he was gone.

"Never mind him," cried Bob Blazes—"He's got important business to attend to, to-night, and can't be with us. Bring out the whiskey, and let's have a talk."

The whiskey was brought; and all the Killers participated therein, save the one who was stretched in the corner on a pile of old carpets.

"To-morrow night is election night, and we may as well make a raise before we go." Thus spoke Bob Blazes, and his sentiments were greeted with a chorus of oaths.

"To make a long story short, boys, to-morrow night, a rich nabob of Walnut street, who has failed for $200,000, and who carries a great part of his money about him—for fear of his creditors, who could lay hold of houses or lands if he owned either—to-morrow night, this nabob comes down to the groggery, in Dog Alley, kept by the big nigger —"

"The Bulgine! D—n him," said ten voices in a breath.

"He's coming there on some dirty work. Now I move that we set a portion of our gang to raise the devil among the niggers of Mary street, while we watch for the nabob, and get hold of him, and bring him to our den."

This sentiment met with an unanimous response. Placing the candle on the floor, Bob squatted beside it, and motioned to the others to follow his example. Presently a circle of "gallows" faces surrounded the light, with the sunburnt and scarred visage of Bob Blazes in the centre.

As for the solitary Killer, he still reclined on his couch of old carpets—apparently overcome with rum or sleep.

"He carries some two or three thousand dollars about him," said Bob. "His name is—never mind his name. Now follow my directions. You, Bill, will take care and get a police officer or two to help our gang to raise a muss among the niggers. You, Jake, will head half of the boys, and first raise an alarm of fire. You, Tom, will come with me, and hang around the groggery in Dog Alley, tomorrow night, after dark. And as for you, Sam, you'd better see Hickory Parchment, the Politician, and get him to wink at our little muss— that is if we do raise a muss. Now let's understand one another—"

And while he laid down before this Senate of the Killers, his plan of operations for the Mexican Campaign of the ensuing night, the shouts of the banqueting Killers, in the next room, came through the partition, like the yells of so many Congressmen engaged in getting up a fight on the last day of the session.

At length the matter was clearly understood. Deep in whiskey, the ten Killers shouted hurrah! at every other word of their leader, while the eleventh lay upon his bed of old carpets in one corner.

His evident inattention to the business in contemplation at length aroused the curiosity of Bob Blazes, the Leader.

"Who's that snoring there in the corner," he asked.

"It's only Lije—Lije Watson, who's just got out o' the Penitenshery," answered one of the eleven—"He was in for passin' counterfeit money—you know, I told you all about it the other day. He's a little drunk, I guess."

"Not so drunk as you think," answered that peculiarly husky voice, which we have heard before, "'Not drunk, only reflectin',' as Judge Tomahawk said when the Temperance Society waited on him, to thank him for his temperance speeches and found him drunk."

And as he said this, Elijah arose from his pile of carpets, and squatted down in the midst of the Killers, directly opposite their Leader.

"Drink somethin', Lije," cried one—"You're pale as thunder."

"What makes your eyes look so queer?" said another. "Got a touch o' the man with the poker?"

Elijah was indeed frightfully pale. His eyes sunk deep in their sockets, had a wild and glassy look. With his hands laid on his knees, he turned his gaze from face to face, until it rested upon the scarred and sunburnt visage of Bob Blazes, the Leader.

"I've heard your story about this nabob, as you call him, and now I'd like to ask you a question or two," said Elijah.

"Fire away," responded the Leader.

"Did this nabob once live in Walnut street near — street?"

"He did," answered Bob.

"Did he disappear four years ago, and was his hat found on the wharf?"

"You're too hard for me 'Lije," was the answer of the Leader, "I can't answer that. Take a little whiskey, and get some color in your face. You look like a subject on a dissecting table."

"Was his name Jacob D. Z. Hicks?" said Elijah fixing his eyes earnestly upon the Leader, and grasping him rather roughly by the arm.

Bob Blazes dropped the bottle on the floor. He started up and shook the hand of the Discharged Convict from his arm, exclaiming—"Why 'Lije has the manny poker sure enough. Thunder! What puts such ideas into his head? What the devil do I know of your Zebediah Hicks?"

With these words he resumed his seat, in the midst of the band, who assailed Elijah with a burst of laughter, mingled with curses.

"Drink somethin' 'Lije, and drive away the horrors," was the end of their chorus.

Nothing daunted, 'Lije turned his corpselike face to the light, and regarding "Bob Blazes" with the same fixed stare, said slowly—

"Come captain, you need'nt shove me off in that way. It rayther sharpens a man's senses to spend four years in Cherry Hill, and I'm jist possessed by the idea—I don't know why, and I don't keer why—that your rich nabob is nobody else than Hicks the Merchant, who disappeared four years ago. Now, you know me boys, (surveying the other Killers) and you know that when my blood's up, I am always *thar*. I am. So if you want me to go into your muss, with the right sperrit, tomorrow night, Bob must answer my question. Yes or no! Is your nabob named Jacob D. Z. Hicks?"

"Why do you ask?" said Bob, rather cowed—at least surprised—by the earnest manner of the Convict—"What have you got to do with this Hicks?"

"Nothin' much. Only I was put to jail for passin' a note on one of his Banks, which note happened to be counterfeit. That's all."

"Well," said Bob, drawing a long puff from a cigar, which he had lighted at the candle—"If it's any satisfaction to you to know it, I am induced to believe, that this nabob was once named Jacob D. Z. Hicks"

A flush of red, shot into the cheeks of the Convict. He said nothing, but quietly reached for the bottle, and took a long and hearty draught. After a pause, he said in a careless way to Bob Blazes—

"Come Blazes, you've seen somethin' of life and so have I. Suppose we tell somethin' of our lives to the boys. You begin."

Thus addressed, Blazes stretched himself leisurely along the floor, and punctuating his narrative, with draughts of whiskey and puffs of cigar smoke, told the boys some of the events of his history. His story, interspersed with oaths and slang, still gave some traces in its language of a good collegiate education.

It was a stirring narrative. It spoke much of life in Havana—of life on the coast of Africa—of slave ships stored thick and foul with their miserable cargo—and of the manner in which certain mercantile houses, in the north, made hoards of money, even at the present day, by means of the Slave Trade.

Even the Killers turned away in involuntary loathing, from the recital of the hellish exploits of this man, who only known to them for a few weeks, by the name of "Bob Blazes" had doubtless borne a different and more significant name, in Havana and on the coast of Africa.

After he had done, Elijah commenced.

His was a different story. How, for four years, he had sat in his cell, night and day, day and night, counting every throb of his heart, and wondering whether he should ever put his foot on free ground again. There was something like eloquence in the manner of the Convict. His pale face lighted up, and his eyes shone, and his hands moved in rapid gesticulation—he was telling to these Outcasts, the story of his wretched Life—a brief but harrowing story, commencing with the life of an apprentice at the work bench, and ending with the life of a Convict in the Eastern Penitentiary.

The Killers shuddered—even Bob Blazes, the hero of the Slave Ship felt the tears start to his eyelids.

"And this Jacob D. Z. Hicks was the cause of my bein' sent to Cherry Hill"—thus he concluded his recital—"and so if your nabob turns out to be, Mister Jacob D. Z. Hicks, don't you think I've got an account to settle with him?"

The Killers rather thought he had. And so did Bob.

PART XIV. THE RIOT NEAR "THE CALIFORNIA HOUSE."

The night after these scenes in the Den of the Killers was election night—October—1849. On that night the city and districts of Philadelphia were alive with excitement. Every street had its bonfire; crowds of voters were collected around every poll; bar-room and groggery overflowed with drunken men. The city and the districts were astir. And through the darkness of night, a murmur rose at intervals like the tramp of an immense army.

It was election night. The good citizens were engaged in making a Sheriff who might prove an honest man and a faithful officer, or who might heap up wealth, by stolen fees, and leave the county to riot and murder, while he grew rich upon the misery of the people. The good citizens were also engaged in electing Members of Assembly who might go to Harrisburg and do their duty like men, or who might go there as the especial hirelings of Bank speculators, paid to enact laws that give wealth to one class, and poverty and drunkenness to another. There was a stirring time around the State House: the entire vicinity ran over with patriotism and brandy. Vote for Moggs the People's friend! Vote for Hoggs the sterling patriot! Don't forget Boggs the hero of Squamdog! Appeals like these glared from the placards on the walls, and flashed from the election lanterns,[33] carried in the hands of sturdy politicians. In fine, all over the county, the boys had their bonfires, the men their brandy and politics, the Candidates their agonies of suspense.

There was one District, however, which added a new feature to the excitement of election night. It was that District, which partly comprised in the City Proper, and partly in in[34] Moyamensing, swarms with hovels, courts, groggeries—with dens of every grade of misery and of drunkenness—festering there, thick and rank, as insects in a tainted cheese. It cannot be denied that hard-working and honest people, reside in the Barbarian District. Nor can it be denied that it is the miserable refuge of the largest portion of the Outcast population of Philadelphia county

This District has for two years been the scene of perpetual outrage. Here, huddled in rooms thick with foul air, and drunk on poison that can be purchased for a penny a glass, you may see white and black, young and old, man and woman, cramped together in crowds that fester with wretchedness, disease and crime. This mass of misery and starvation affords a profitable harvest to a certain class of "hangers on of the law" who skulk about the offices of Alderman, trade in licenses and do the dirty work which prominent politicians do not care to do for themselves.

Through this district, at an early hour on the night of election, a furniture car, filled with blazing tar barrels, was dragged by a number of men and boys, who yelled like demons, as they whirled their locomotive bonfire through the streets. It was first taken through a narrow street, known as St. Mary street, and principally inhabited by negroes, and distant about one square from the groggery of the "Bulgine" and the home of the young woman, mentioned in the previous pages. As the car whirled along a shot was fired; a cry at once arose that a white man was killed, and the attention of the mob was directed to a house at the corner of Sixth and St. Mary, kept by a black fellow who (so the rumor ran) was married to a white woman. The mob gathered numbers every moment, and a conflict ensued between the white mob and the negroes who had fortified themselves within the California House (a four story building) and in the neighboring tenements and hovels. The inmates after a desperate contest were forced to fly; the bar was destroyed, and the gas set on fire. In a moment the house was in a blaze and the red light flashing against the sky, was answered by the State House Bell, which summoned the engine and hose companies to the scene of action. The Hope, the Good Will, the Phoenix, the Vigilant and other engine companies arrived upon the scene—amid the clamor of the riot, while pistol shots broke incessantly on the air, and the flames of burning houses ascended to the heavens, lighting with a red glare the faces of the mob—and attempted to save the houses, which were yet untouched by the flames. Their efforts were fruitless. The mob took possession of the Franklin Engine, and ran it up St. Mary street; as for the other companies, they were greeted at every turn by discharges of fire-arms, loaded with buckshot and slugs. Charles Himmelwright, a fireman of the Good Will, was shot through the heart, while nobly engaged in the discharge of his duty. He was a young and honest man. He fell dead the moment he received the shot. Many were wounded, and many killed. It was an infernal scene. The faces of the mob reddened by the glare, the houses whirling in flames, the streets slippery with blood, and a roar like the yells of a thousand tigers let loose upon their prey, all combined, gave the appearance of a sacked and ravaged town, to the District which spreads around Sixth and St. Mary street. The rioters and spectators in the streets were not the only sufferers. Men and women sheltered within their homes, were shot by the stray missiles of the cowardly combatants.

While these scenes were in progress around the California House, all was quiet in Dog Alley. The hovels of the Court were closed or deserted; the place looked as though it had not been oc-cupied for a month. There were indeed two exceptions—a light shone from the greasy windows of the groggery, kept by the Bulg-ine, and another emitted its struggling rays from the home of Mrs. Watson and her daughter Kate.

PART XV. THE BULGINE AND KATE.

Black Andy, *alias*, the Bulgine, was standing at his door, with folded arms, the light from within playing over one side of his face, when footsteps were heard from the farther extremity of the Court, and a female figure was seen approaching through the gloom. It was the poor girl, Kate Watson, "the supernumerary," on her way to the theatre. With her shawl thrown over her shoulders, and her veil drooping over her face, she came along with a hesitating step, pausing every moment as if to listen to the noise of the conflict which was progressing at the distance of not more than two hundred yards.

On she came; the light from the groggery shone over her tall form; she paused, when a hand was laid upon her mouth, and her arms were pinioned to her side, by an arm that encircled her with a grasp of iron. She struggled, as if for life, but the iron arm held her arms firmly against her sides. She attempted to scream, but in vain. Tossing back her head in her struggles, she beheld with a horror that no words can paint, the black visage of the negro.

It may be as well to observe that the events of the night had in some measure changed the plan of "the Gentleman," otherwise called "the Manager," and the negro. Instead of stationing the cab at the corner of the Court, they had placed it in a neighboring street, which communicated with the back door of the groggery, by means of a narrow alley. Therefore, Black Andy bore the struggling girl into his bar room, and from the bar room into a room on the second story, where waited the Gentleman, anxious to comfort his victim ere he had her conveyed to the cab. He designed to have her kept within this room until the mob would reach its heighth, when the additional confusion would serve to render his passage to a mansion in the heart of the city at once convenient and safe. The negro ascended the stairs, applied a bit of rag, wet with some pungent liquid, to the lips of the girl, and the next moment tumbled her insensible form into the room, where the Gentleman waited for him.

The liquid was chloroform. The Gentleman had provided it for the fulfilment of his plans, and given it to the Bulgine.

This accomplished, the negro descended, hurried along the alley to see that the cab stood there, in the street, according to the plan agreed upon. He then returned to his bar room, which he had entirely cleared of its usual customers an hour before. Busying himself behind the bar, he was surprised by the entrance of the "Loafer" in the grey rags, whom he had ejected the night previous. In his African dialect, he bade the fellow quit his premises; but the Loafer whined piteously for a glass of whiskey, which the Bulgine at last consented to give him.

As he poured out the liquid poison, the Loafer leaned over the counter, one hand on a large earthen pitcher, supposed to contain water.

"Dar yer whiskey. Take it and trabel," said the Bulgine, pushing the glass toward his customer. The Loafer raised his glass slowly to his lips, and at the same time kept one hand upon the handle of the pitcher, but instead of drinking the poison, he dashed it in the negro's eyes, at the same time hurling the pitcher, with all the force of his arm, at his head. Blinded by the liquor, half stunned by the blow, the Bulgine uttered a frightful howl, and attempted to strike his antagonist across the bar. But a second blow, administered with a "slung shot,"[35] which the Loafer drew from his rags, took the negro on the forehead and laid him flat upon the floor.

The moment that he fell, the room was filled with "Killers," who surrounded their Leader, known as the "Loafer" or Bob Blazes, with shouts and cries. They were eleven in number, whom Bob had instructed the night before. Drunken, furious, and brutal, they were about to beat and mangle the prostrate negro, when Bob stopped them with a word:

"Look here, boys! The devil's delight is up in St. Mary street, and we must be busy while the fun lasts. Four of you go to the end of the alley, and take care of the cab; two of you guard the front door, and let the rest remain outside, on the watch, while I go up stairs. When I whistle ALL come. I'll go up and see the old fellow and his gal."

He was implicitly obeyed. Four of the Killers hastened through the back door; two remained in the bar-room, (Elijah Watson was one of the two) and the rest went out into the court. Pausing for a moment, ere he ascended the dark stairway, Bob wiped from his hands the blood which he had received in the conflict near the California House—for he had been in the thickest of the fight, at the moment when Himmelwright fell. Then casting a look toward the prostrate form of the negro stretched behind the door, his forehead covered with blood, Bob whispered to Elijah, who, pale and trembling, leaned against the Bar. He then crept up the stairs, and placed his ear against the door at the head of the flight. All was still within. Bob pushed open the door and entered. By the light of a tallow candle, the "Gentleman" with hair and whiskers well oiled, his hat and overcoat thrown aside, was contemplating the form of the insensible girl, who was stretched upon a miserable bed.

Her hair fell in disorder about her neck—her eyes were closed and her lips parted; she looked extremely beautiful, but it was a beauty like death. And over her, his false hair looking quite glossy in the light, stood the aged sinner, his eyes fixed upon his unconscious victim, and his eyes parted in a singular but meaning smile.

The noble form of the poor girl was stretched before him—in his power—in a few hours she would be safe within his mansion in the heart of the City. Thus occupied he had not heard the opening of the door, nor was he aware of the presence of Bob, until that personage laid a hand upon his arm, saying mildly:

"How d'ye do, father."

PART XVI. THE FATHER AND SON.

The surprise of the Gentleman may be imagined.

Turning, he beheld that stalwart figure, clad in rags which were stained with blood. The cap, drawn over the brows, concealed the upper part of the whiskered face. The Gentleman could not believe his ears. He started as though he had received a musquet[36] shot.

As for Bob, he removed his cap.

"Good evening, father," he said, with a bland smile, "How have you been these four years? You really look much younger than when I saw you last. Drowning seems to agree with you. And *when* did you hear from mother? Has the gay old lady departed from this scene of sublunary care, or has she married Sir Charles? Upon my word, you don't seem a bit rejoiced to see your long lost son. Come, shall we kill the fatted calf, or shall we give each other a real French hug? What, still silent? Well, old gentleman, I've been told that you was dying to see me about that five thousand which I got cashed for you. Here I am. Now what do you want with me?"

Mr. Jacob D. Z. Hicks was dumb. He could not speak—in sober verity, he had not the power to frame a word. (The "Gentleman," otherwise called the "English Manager," was indeed our old friend Jacob D. Z. Hicks, who, after his death by drowning, had been spending a few years abroad, enjoying himself pleasantly, upon the proceeds of the Broken Banks.) He now stood with his back to the only window of the miserable apartment, his hands behind him, and his eyes fixed in a sort of stupid wonder upon the form of the "Prodigal Son," Bob Blazes, *alias* CROMWELL HICKS.

"Come, father," said Cromwell, drawing the back of his right hand across his scarred face—"This really wont do. You mus really—" Crom made great use of the word really—"You must really kill the fatted calf for your Prodigal Son—or stay—you have a belt about your waist, containing some gold and bank notes. Hand it over, if you please. I've been in rough scenes since you kicked me out of the store, and am apt to get cross when people don't mind what I say. Hand it over, I say. Strip!"

He advanced a step nearer.

Mr. Jacob D. Z. Hicks, crouching against the window, unbuttoned his vest, and took from beneath it, a leathern belt which, to all seeming, contained a considerable amount in specie.

"It's all I have in the world. Take that, and I'm a beggar," he faltered.

Cromwell coolly reached forth his hand to take the belt, exclaiming, "The belt belongs to me, and as for this pretty girl, whom you are going to take to your mansion in the city, why Don Jorge, the son of Captain VELAZQUEZ—you mind the name?—will take care of her. He has the key of your mansion, and is now down stairs in the guise of a Killer."

If the good Jacob D. Z. Hicks had turned pale at the sight of his supposed son, he grew livid at the very name of Captain Velasquez.

He handed the belt without a word. Cromwell took it—glanced at the form of the unconscious girl—and then turned to the door—

"Hallo! Don Jorge, I say! You're wanted up here! Leave Lije in the bar room and come up!"

This said, Cromwell opened the belt (with the key which Mr. Hicks had handed to him) and proceeded to ascertain the amount which it contained. Bending toward the light, he was thus occupied, when Mr. Jacob D. Z. Hicks heard a step on the stairway, and saw a form in the door. In the slim gentleman, disguised in the rough garb of a Killer, you will recognize our friend Don Jorge, whose dark-hued face, black hair and whiskers, show to advantage under his round-rimmed hat.

"The son of Velasquez!" ejaculated Hicks.

"Good evening to you, friend of my father," said Don Jorge, advancing, "I am glad to see you, though you didn't exactly treat the old man well, when, nearly five years ago, his vessel (and yours) was seized off the Brazil coast. You left Velasquez to rot in jail, on the charge of piracy, while you, safe in Philadelphia, fingered the proceeds of his former ventures. Velasquez has been free some years—that is, free from the world. He was hanged like a dog on one of the British Islands. You had reaped a fortune from his zeal in the slave trade, but when the hour came for you to help him, you sat quiet in Philadelphia, and let him hang. But his son has been on your track. He stands before you."

His dark eyes gleaming vengeance, he drew near the affrighted man, who trembled in every nerve.

"Yes, father," said Cromwell, looking up for a moment, as he counted the money and laid a portion of it upon the table—"It's all true. And at the very time when you kicked me from the store, Don

Jorge (who had been placed at Yale College by his father) heard of his father's death. We left college together, and—"

"I had determined to be revenged upon you through your son, when I first left college," interrupted Don Jorge—"But when I discovered that your son was *not* your son, why I opened my plans fully to him, and we sailed together in the Sara Jane, which had been purchased for me by friends of my dead father—not such friends as you, by Heaven! And now, sir, after some years of stirring adventure, on land and on sea, we have come to this city together, and our main object has been to see you. By the bye, we tracked you from Paris to Liverpool, and from Liverpool to Philadelphia. We are here together, your son and the son of Velasquez What have you to say for yourself?"

"And it's what I call an agreeable coincidence," said Cromwell, placing the money in the belt and locking it again, "Five thousand dollars! This isn't enough, old man."

Had the thousands of widows and orphans, who had been robbed by Hicks as the Banker, have seen him now they would have been amply revenged.

Crouching against the window, (whose frame he clutched with hands behind his back) the Ex-Banker exhibited a grotesque and yet pitiful picture of affright. His eye rolled as he surveyed by turns, the scarred face of Cromwell, and the swarthy visage of the Son of Velasquez.

"Come, my friend, you must let us have more than this," said Cromwell advancing.

"Where do you keep all your money?" interrupted Don Jorge also advancing—"I searched your house in —— street tonight, searched it through and through, but couldn't find a dollar."

"Gentlemen," gasped the Ex-Banker, "have some pity upon an old man—"

"As you pitied me, when you called me a bastard and kicked me from the store," and Cromwell drew a knife from beneath his rags.

"As you pitied my father when you left him to the gallows," and thus speaking Don Jorge drew a "revolver" from the pocket of his coat.

Certainly the tide had turned against Mr. Jacob D. Z. Hicks.

"The devil's up in the city to-night, and men have been shot, who are worth your weight in gold," thus spoke Cromwell—"One man wouldn't be missed much—particularly a man like you. What say you Don Jorge shall we 'fix him' off in this snug room, and then take the girl to his house and cast lots for her?"

"The girl shall go with us, at all events, but as for him, his life depends upon a word. Will you tell us where your money is concealed? Yes or No?"

Mr. Jacob D. Z. Hicks fell on his knees, while Don Jorge presented the pistol at his throat. The girl, meanwhile, under the influence of chloroform, lay quiet as death upon the bed.

"Yes or No!"

Again Don Jorge spoke these words, and stood over the Ex-Banker, his eyes flashing with the long indulged lust of vengeance.

PART XVII. ELIJAH THE CONVICT AND KILLER.

But at this moment a new actor appeared upon the scene. It was Elijah Watson, who pale and trembling had crept up-stairs, and now stood on the threshold, his sunken eyes shining with a sinister light, as he surveyed the face of the kneeling man. He did not see the girl who was stretched insensible on the bed, nor was he aware that the victim of the intended outrage was his *almost* sister, his sister in everything, but the tie of blood—Kate Watson.

Without seeming to notice either Cromwell or Don Jorge, Elijah advanced, his shabby apparel shown in the candle light, as he clenched a "slung shot" in his right hand. Hicks saw his face, but did not at first recognize in that visage, distorted by despair, the countenance of Elijah Watson, which he had seen four years before through the aperture in the Penitentiary wall.

Elijah advanced, his steps making scarcely an audible sound, until beside Don Jorge he confronted the kneeling man. His breath came hot and gasping through his clenched teeth. The effects of the liquor with which he had deadened his senses, passed away like a flash, as soon as he found himself in the presence of Jacob D. Z. Hicks—HIS FATHER.

"Is this Jacob Hicks?" he said in a voice whose unnatural emphasis made Don Jorge start, and caused something like a chill to run through Cromwell's veins.

"It is the man, but why don't you keep watch down stairs?" said Cromwell.

"The black fellow may revive—you should be on the watch," added Don Jorge. (Be it observed that the figure of Cromwell, cast a broad shadow over the form of the insensible girl.)

"Is your name Jacob Hicks? Jacob D. Z. Hicks?" asked Elijah bending down, until the Ex-Banker felt his breath upon his cheek.

"It is—that is—ah"—faltered Hicks, endeavoring in vain to call to mind the place and the time, in which he had seen that face before.

"And you came and peeped at me through the hole in the Penitentiary wall," gasped Elijah—"You did, and went away again, knowin' that I was your son. You looked at me and left me to four years of days and nights in that stone coffin"—

He raised the slung shot, as though he would crush the skull of the kneeling man, while Don Jorge and Cromwell stood vacant-eyed and wonder-stricken at his words, but even as the blow was about to fall, Hicks shrieked, in a voice whose accent of pitiful fright was painful to hear—

"It is Elijah! It is my son! Elijah, I saw you, four years ago, but could not relieve you. Hear me, and then—if you can—kill your father. There, at your shoulder, stands the man who has for twenty-three years cheated you out of the rights of a son, while you were cast an outcast on the world. That man's mother, also your mother and my wife, gave you birth twenty-three years ago, and sent you out into the world without father or name, while her bastard occupied your place by my hearthstone. You, the real son, was condemned to poverty and want, while he, the child of adultery, took your place, and from the petted boy became the profligate man. Listen, Elijah—listen—you must hear me."

And Jacob D. Z. Hicks clutched the Convict by the knees, and told him, in rapid and broken tones, the real story of his parentage. Cromwell's face displayed all the changes of wonder and hatred—wonder at the revelation, and hatred equally divided between Hicks and Elijah. As for Don Jorge, he listened and burst into a roar of laughter—

"I vow," he cried, with a Spanish oath, "It's as good as a play. If they'd only sing it, we should have an Opera on the spot!"

"Well met, father and son,"—and Cromwell advanced, his scarred face swollen with rage—"The father, a bankrupt merchant, a man who is ashamed to bear his own name—the son, a 'number' from the Penitentiary! Embrace your daddy, Lije! You're welcome to him!"

"You hear him—you will protect me?" cried Hicks, clutching the knees of the Convict.

Elijah was silent. His lips writhed over his set teeth; there was a swelling of the chords of his throat; the slung-shot fell with his right hand to his side.

"And yet you could look through the wall—and see me sittin' in the cell—and know that I was put there for passin' a counterfeit on one of your banks—and go away and leave me! You could!"

Was it a tear that rolled down his sunken cheek?

"He did—he saw you there, and left you," cried Cromwell, now anxious to inflame the Convict against Hicks—"He made a Convict of you, and that's a fact!"

Elijah turned and looked steadily upon the form of his "false" Brother. He surveyed him from head to foot, while his eyes seemed to sink deeper into their sockets, and his lips parted in a spasmodic grimace—

"Bah! I'd sooner herd with all the Convicts of the Eastern Penitentiary, than to own a man like you for brother, or a thing like *that* for father. Go at one another—come! He's a swindlin' bank director, and you're a slave pirate—you'll just suit. I'm only a Convict. I'm not good enough company for you two."

At these words Don Jorge burst into a fresh peal of laughter; Cromwell grew red with rage; the ex-merchant did not relax his hold upon the Convict's knees.

"You miserable felon, do you dare to use such language to *me*? To ME?"

Thus speaking, Cromwell advanced with the knife; Elijah folded his arms, and regarded him with a broad grin upon his pale face. The composed attitude of the Convict—his head, with its short black hair and protuberant forehead, set firmly on his shoulders—seemed to disconcert the "Slaver," otherwise known as the Leader of the Killers.

"Why don't you strike? Do you think that a man who has stood four years in a stone coffin is afraid of a thing like you? You can play the devil with niggers—I don't doubt that. But you daresent strike me!"

Cromwell did strike—it was a swift and terrible blow—but the Convict knocked up his arm, and forced him back upon the bed, his hand clutching the throat of his "false" brother, until that brother's face grew livid as the visage of a dying man. Then, as he held him writhing on the bed, he for the first time beheld the motionless form and death-like face of Kate.

"It's Kate!" he shouted, and pressed her hands. They were cold. Her eyes were shut. There was no breath in her nostrils—no motion in her pulseless bosom. With her flowing brown hair, and magnificent form, she looked very beautiful, but her beauty was the beauty of death.

"Who's done this?" cried Elijah, rushing to Don Jorge, then to Hicks, and last of all to Cromwell, who stood gasping for breath, the print of the Convict's fingers yet fresh upon his throat—"Who, I say? Who's killed that girl? We aint brother and sister by blood, but we are brother and sister by the years of poverty and starvation we've passed together. Feel her hands—they're like ice. Look at her—I swear she's dead and one of you has killed her."

At these words, uttered with every accent of an agony that was like madness, the three listeners could not repress an ejaculation of horror.

Cromwell rushed to the bed—"She is dead, by —!" he cried with an oath. Don Jorge followed him, and even Hicks, pale and shaking, drew near the miserable couch whereon she was stretched in her deathly loveliness.

"Dead!" cried Jorge—and felt her cold hands.

Hicks could only ejaculate the word "Chloroform."

Hicks could not frame a word, but sank helplessly upon the bed, not from remorse so much, as from a terror of the results of this scene.

The convict now presented a terrible picture. Tearing away the coat from his neck, as though it choked him, he clutched the slung shot, and looked into every face—his limbs trembling as with the impulse of a madman's strength.

"Who did this?" he said, in a voice that resembled the cry of a drowning man.

"This man—with Chloroform," answered Cromwell, retreating from the mad stare of the convict—"He hired the nigger to bring her up here, and the nigger poisoned her with Chloroform. I overheard them talking about their plans last night—"

Elijah took the candle, and bent over the bed, surveying the face of the dead girl. Her eyelashes rested dark and distinct upon her colorless cheeks—her lips were parted disclosing her clear white teeth—her noble bust, from which the shawl had been tossed aside, was motionless in death. How the convict bent over her and crushed her hands in his rough fingers, and spoke to her by name—how he raised her from the bed, only to see her fall back, motionless and dead again—how he, in his mad way, endeavored to call her back to life by reminding her of the years of want and suffering they had passed together—we need not picture it.

While he was thus engaged Cromwell buckled the money belt about his waist, and beckoned to Don Jorge. They passed with noiseless step to the door, and Cromwell took the key from the lock. In a moment they had passed the threshold, and Cromwell having placed the key in the lock, in the outside, was about closing the door, when Hicks—his wig cast aside—darted forward and endeavored to leave the room.

Cromwell said nothing, but as the Ex-broker came he planted a blow on his forehead, which sent him spinning back into the room. This done, he closed the door and locked it on the outside, remarking to his comrade in a whisper—

"We'll leave 'em there together. The room has but one window and the shutters are nailed fast, and as for the door I've got the key in my pocket. Come—let us go down stairs, and give the Killers the slip, while we go up and search Hicks' house in the city. We'll search it once more. His money is *there*. I'm sure of it. By the bye, they'll have a good time of it in there, the father, the son and the dead girl!"

He spoke as they stood in the darkness at the head of the stairs, which led down into the bar room. They could see the light from the bar room, shining upon the foot of the stairs.

"Still it's bad about that girl," said Don Jorge in a voice that was agitated by a tremor.

They descended the narrow stairway, Cromwell going first.

"Yes, we'll leave 'em up there together, while we go and search the old man's house," he said as they reached the foot of the stairs—

"Then when we have all his money, why hurrah for Cuba! I say Don Jorge—"

Half turning toward his companion, who was still in the dark, Cromwell with one side of his face touched by the light, placed his foot upon the threshold. At that moment, a cry was heard, and an hand striking from the bar room, descended upon Cromwell's breast. Don Jorge saw the blow, and thought he saw the flash of a knife; the next thing that he saw was the body of Cromwell falling forward into the bar room, with a heavy sound.

It was but a step to the door—Don Jorge rushed forward—and as his way was blocked by the quivering body of his friend—he saw the giant negro standing in the bar room, not a foot from the head of Cromwell, his hideous face overspread with a grin of triumph, and a huge knife glittering in his uplifted hand. That knife glittered with the life blood of Cromwell. The negro, during the absence of the Killers, had recovered from the effects of the blow—had procured the knife— and waited behind the door, as he heard the steps of Cromwell upon the stairs. He had struck but once; the blow was sufficient. Prostrate on his face, the blood from the wound trickling over the boards of the floor, Cromwell quivered for a moment like a man suspended on a gibbet—made a grasp at the floor with his hands—and then was quiet and motionless. He never spoke again.

And over him, triumphant and chuckling stood the negro, "*Bulgine*"—the knife which he shook, dripping its red drops, upon his black and brawny arm.

"Come on you dam Killer," he shouted—"I gib you some more ob de same sort. Hah, yah, y-a-h! You strike a nigger do you? Come on!"

In his rage, he planted his foot upon the back of the dead man's head, and showing his broad black chest, awaited the approach of Don Jorge. The Cuban had seen much of blood in his time, but this scene horrified him in every nerve. He felt for his revolver—it was not in its usual place, under his vest—he had left it in the room above. Unarmed, defenceless, he was at the mercy of the giant, whose brute strength, was sufficient to grind him to powder, Could he rush past the Bulgine and gain the den which led into the alley? Or should he endeavor to escape by the back way, and make good his retreat, into the next street?

Not much time was allowed him for thought. Seeing that he did not advance, and reasoning from his hesitation that he was either afraid or unarmed, the Negro sprang toward him, trampling the body of Cromwell beneath his feet.

"Come to me, if you dar, you dam Killer tief!" he cried—Don Jorge saw the knife—sprang backward, and felt a door give way behind him. He gathered himself up, and in an instant was out of the back door, and pursuing his way through the narrow alley which led into the public street. The negro did not follow him. And thus leaving Cromwell to his fate, Don Jorge passed into the street, avoided the crowd, and made the best of his way to the mansion of Mr. Hicks, in the city. He did not recognize a single Killer in the crowds which he encountered; they had been attracted from their watch at the end of the alley by other and more stirring scenes.

As for the Killers who had been stationed in front of the groggery in Dog Alley, they had been led from their posts, soon after Cromwell went up stairs. The riot had rolled its waves of tumult and blood from the California House to Dog Alley. While Cromwell lay dead in the bar room, it had reached its heighth. Firemen, Negroes, and Killers were mingled together in the dense crowd which now blocked up the wide street at the end of Dog Alley—their faces reddened by the glare which came from a burning house. Pistol shots were heard, mingled with the yell of riot and the short quick cry of dying men. While the Negroes and the Killers, penned up in the dense crowd, maintained their conflict, the firemen nobly endeavored to do their duty and extinguish the flames of the burning house. They were attacked by portions of the mob, and the riot only grew more desperate and bloody. It was a battle in all its bloodshed—a battle stripped of the glare of military glory—a mere vulgar affair of butchery and murder, carried on by men whom rum and blood had transformed into devils.

PART XVIII. THE BULGINE AT BAY.

When the riot in the street was at its highest, a small body of the rioters separated from the scene, and plunged into Dog Alley, which, so near the scene of uproar, was all quiet and dark.

"Let's git Bob Blazes and go at 'em again!" cried the foremost of these rioters, and, ten in number, they hastened to the groggery and poured into its door.

"Come on, you dam Killers!"—a voice saluted them—"Come on, you dam tief!"—and they beheld the Bulgine, half naked, standing in one corner, the knife in his hand and his foot upon the dead body of Cromwell.

Furious with liquor and riot, the comrades of Cromwell (known to them as Bob Blazes) recoiled in horror at the sight.

Cromwell's face was upturned, the eyes glaring and the lips distorted.

The Killers raised a shout, rushed forward, but the negro was ready for them. Bracing himself in the corner, his foot planted on the breast of the dead man, he answered their shout as they came on, and described a terrible circle before his breast with the blade of his bloody knife.

"Git some powder and lead!"—cried one of the band—"I'd like to wing him as he stands there: go, Bill, and be quick about it—"

But another of the band made a suggestion in a whisper, which was received with great satisfaction. This suggestion made, the Killers retired in a body, leaving the negro alone with the dead man. A portion of their number attained the rear of the groggery, and effectually closed and fastened the back door, while the others nailed and secured the door and window which opened on Dog Alley.

In a few moments the groggery was in flames.

How it was done it is not necessary to relate; but as the flames burst upon the darkness of the alley, the conflict in the neighboring street came like a wave of fists and clubs, and faces stamped with frenzy, to the very door of the burning hovel. Chased like dogs before the hounds into the alley, a number of negroes beheld themselves between the clubs and pistols of the Killers and the fury of the flames. The combat was renewed; negroes and whites were fighting in the narrow court, and the flames, mounting to the roof, began to communicate with the adjoining hovels—yes, with the flames which ascended from the house which stood in the next street.

At this period a sound was heard which chilled a thousand hearts with involuntary terror.

That sound resounded from the midst of the flames. It was like the howl of a wild beast at bay.

"There's a man in that house!" roared a number of voices in chorus.

"Let him burn!" answered one of the Killers, as his face, streaked with dirt and blood, was reddened by the flames.

The sound was heard again, and as a thousand eyes were uplifted, there appeared on the roof of the groggery a huge dark form, environed by flames, and bearing the form of a woman in his arms. She was insensible, perchance dead—her dress fluttered in a puff of air as he held her aloft in his brawny arms—and his black face, reddened by the flames, was seen beneath the form which he held on high. Seen for a moment only, for a cloud of smoke rolled over him, and he disappeared.

Then a cry rose from the crowd—negroes and whites, firemen and Killers—spectators at distant windows—that you would not have forgotten in a life-time.

The cloud of smoke had rolled away, and—

There, on the very edge of the roof, stood the negro, his half-naked frame raised to its full height, as he raised the body of the girl above his head, straining his arms as though he was about to dash himself and his burden upon the heads of the multitude

"Save the gal!"

"Bring a ladder!"

"Go into the next house and get on the roof—you may help her thar!"

"Go it, Killers!"

"Down with the niggers!"

Cries like these were heard amid the tumult of the crowd, and then a black cloud swept the negro and his burden suddenly from the sight. The next instant a rumor spread among the Killers—originated we cannot tell how—that Elijah Watson was shut up in the burning house. Neither can we tell why the fact had not been thought of before; possibly the rioters had been so much engaged in their arduous duties that they had not time to think of him.

"Save Lije!" cried one of the band, "we can get on to the roof of the next house, and catch hold of him somehow. Boys! Hurray for Lije!"

The roof of the adjoining house—we mean the one on the left, as yet untouched by flames—was some feet higher than the roof of the groggery.

PART XIX. HICKS, ELIJAH AND KATE.

Leaving the scene of clamor and excitement, we will go back in our narrative to the moment when Cromwell locked the door, thus imprisoning Elijah and Hicks, and shutting them up within thick walls with the body of the dead girl.

Elijah was endeavoring, in his rude way, to restore the insensible girl to life—chafing her hands and calling her by name—when the harsh sound of the key turning in the lock struck on his ear. Raising his head, he saw the door fast closed, and poor Hicks in a half prostrate position, his bald head visible, and his glossy wig dangling from one ear. Confused by the blow administered by Cromwell, just before he locked the door, Hicks was engaged in raising himself to his feet, meanwhile rubbing his forehead with his right hand. Hicks was by no means the smooth and smiling gentleman we beheld last night, with well-oiled wig and whiskers, spotless shirt bosom and diamond pin. His whiskers had shared the fate of his wig; the diamond pin had fallen; and a spot of blood from his forehead stained the spotless white of his shirt bosom. Certainly, Mr. Hicks looked the very picture of a defeated candidate the day after election.

"What's the matter with you, old man?" said Elijah, taking some pity upon the disconsolate condition of Mr. Hicks.

"They're gone—" began Hicks.

"Who keers?" quoth Elijah.

"But they've locked the door, and—" he cast his eyes toward the dead body of Kate Watson.

"Left me and you together, alone with the corpse," answered Elijah, with a frightful grin, "Look at the winder, Hicks—it's nailed shut. Try the door—the panels are thick, and you can't get it open for your life. Do you think I'd open it for you? No, Hicks, you must come here, and sit one side o' the corpse while I sit on the other, and tell me what you think o' yourself. Come. What! you won't?"

With a scowl and an oath, Elijah advanced upon the kneeling man, and dragged him to the bed. He forced him down upon it, and then seated himself—the body of Kate between them—and the candle-light showing the three faces—Elijah's pale and malignant, Hicks' pale and ashy with terror—the dead girl's pale and very beautiful.

"Jist feel her hands"—he forced the ex banker to take the hand of the dead girl within his own—"how could you do it?"

It was a singular scene. That lone room in a den of pollution—door locked and window nailed—the body of the dead girl upon the bed, and the Convict Son accusing the Rich Father of the Murder. Hicks was terribly agitated, not only on account of the sudden death of Kate Watson, but by reason of the strange light which flashed from the eye of his Felon Son.

'I didn't mean to do it," he faltered, "I told the black fellow to put the wet rag to her lips, so as to render her insensible for a few moments—"

"And what did you *intend* to do with her?" was the next question. It was a puzzling question, but Hicks endeavored to meet it.

"To do her a service—to—to—bring her out upon the stage. Since my failure I have been on the best terms with the English Managers—I could have made her fortune—"

"Father, you lie!" was the response of Elijah, "You know what you intended to make of her; and after all you'd a-left her to die in the streets, as you left me to die in the Penitentiary. Why, when I see you there, and see this poor dead girl stretched between us, and hear you lyin' in that way, I wish myself back again in jail. You're enough to make a whole State's Prison blush."

As he said this, Hicks turned his eyes aside—he could not meet that steady gaze.

"I've half a notion to kick open that den and hand you to the police, and see how you like a few years in Cherry Hill. Then I'd come, ha, ha, ha—hee! I'd come and have a *peep* at you—jist a *p-e-e-p* through the hole in the wall!"

In a voice perfectly cold with fright, Hicks begged for mercy. He reminded Elijah that it was not his fault, that he had been condemned to a life of misery and degradation. He spoke of his wealth—wealth hidden in his city mansion—and offered to share it with his convict son.

"Only get me out of this difficulty—release me from this room—let us go together—if I don't keep my word, why then deliver me to the police for—for—murder!

Elijah reflected.

He played absently with the hand of the deceased girl.

He parted the glossy brown hair aside from her white forehead.

"You consent?" whispered Hicks.

"How much money have you got?" asked Elijah meditatively.

"Twenty thousand in gold—it's hid in my house—no one knows of it but myself—you know I'm in the city under an assumed name—and if you consent we'll leave it to-morrow—leave it together, and—"

"What of *her?*"—Elijah laid his hand over the face of the dead girl. Hicks' visage fell.

"What of *her?*"—There was no answering that.

Elijah rose and stalked up and down the floor, his hands behind his back and his head on his breast, while Hicks, shuddering and cold, removed himself as far as possible from the corse, without actually falling off the bed.

"Where is the money?" said Elijah, turning abruptly in his walk.

Hicks answered in a quiet whisper, and described the location of the house and of the money.

"Give me the key?"

With a shaking hand Hicks drew a key from his vest pocket. Elijah buried it in the pocket of his shabby coat, and then gently lifting Kate's body tore the ragged quilt from the bed, and proceeded with the aid of a clasp knife to divide it into slips.

"Put your hands behind your back—" and Elijah fixed his eye upon the trembling sinner.

Hicks consented like a child. Elijah bound his hands firmly, with two of the strips.

"Stick out your feet." Hicks complied, and in a moment his ankles were bound.

"Now it will take me just half an hour to go to your house and back. You can remain quiet here alongside o' Kate, as your intentions were good—and you need not be afraid of the *body* you know? I'll come back in half an hour, and then if you have told me a lie, I'll—"

Hicks waits with much anxiety for the conclusion of the sentence.

"Then I'll tell you what I'll do."

"You are not going to leave me here, in this condition?" cried the ex-broker, the cold sweat glistening on his forehead—"O for mercy sake I beg—I beg—"

Elijah seized a fragment of an old chair, and with one blow demolished the sash of the window; it was the work of a few moments to make an opening in the boards without. Sturdily brandishing the chair leg, he knocked away the lower boards and looked out. "Opens on a shed! Good!" He placed his hand on the window sill, and looked over his shoulder—"Keep cool, Hicks," he said, and again that rightful grimace came over his face. The next moment he was gone. His foot-steps were heard upon the boards of the shed—there was a sound like a man leaping down upon the solid earth—and then all was quiet.

Hicks found himself alone with the dead. Could he have moved his arms or limbs, he would have placed as great a distance as might be, between himself and the bed, but there he was, pinioned like a "sheep for the slaughter," the body of Kate by his side—nay one of her hands touched his knee. He could just stir, but he could not remove himself from the bed. The candle stood on the floor, flinging its smoky light over the naked walls, and upward into his face. He looked over his right shoulder—the pale face of Kate was there, hair streaming to the shoulders, and the cold beauty of death upon every lineament. The candle begins to sputter in the socket. What if it goes out and leaves him in darkness, and with the dead hand upon his knee? Hark! There are shouts in the room below. Some one is coming to his rescue. He cares not who it is, only so that he is relieved from his horrible position. The sound of a scuffle is heard—they are coming—they are coming! Still no hand unlocks the door. Half dead with terror—Hicks hears voices in the yard—

"Bar the doors, and let's burn the nigger in his den!"

Hicks utters a frightful howl, and then the candle goes out. No! It flashes up again, and flings a horrible light over the room, and upon the face of the dead. Then the candle does indeed go out and all is darkness.

"Help! Help! Murder! Murder!"

But no one hears him. There is the trampling of feet in the yard, and shouts as of a thousand men in the alley—his voice is drowned. Still he shouts and screams until he is hoarse, and his voice can only raise into a half coherent murmur.

The dead body is still by his side. He cannot see it, but he feels the hand upon his knee.

Now a new fear assails him. There is the smell of fire, and the room seems rapidly filling with smoke. He breathes with difficulty. The noise of flames, now mingles with the tramp of feet and the yell of the mob.

Suddenly a red light flashes in the window. The rioters have fired the shed—it burns—it burns—and the smoke whirls in, through the aperture in the boards. The boards catch next and with a desperate effort, the wretched man starts to his feet, only to fall, at full length upon the floor.

At this instant a noise is heard—it is in the room—it completes the terrors of the miserable man—

"O! the bell has rung for the first act, and I am late"—

It is the voice of the poor supernumerary, who reviving from the death-like stupor engendered by Chloroform, now imagines herself once more in the Theatre. She is not dead, for the Chloroform, well nigh fatal, only produced for a while the appearance of death. But Hicks prostrate on his face, does not think of her as living—he is sure that he hears the voice of a ghost. Alas, poor Hicks! Was ever fraudulent Bank Director so horribly visited as you are now?

"Is it a dream?" cries Kate, as she awakes from the delicious frenzy of Chloroform and finds herself environed by flames—the roaring in her ears—the red light in her face—"Has the Theatre taken fire?"

She bounds from the bed—and sees the prostrate form—at the sight, she remembers how the hand of the Negro was fixed upon her mouth, and how he bore her up stairs in the darkness.

"Are you living?" she shrieks—"Speak? What does this mean? Am I to be burned alive?"

To which the unfortunate Hicks, responds as he rubs his face over the floor:

"Cut my feet!" (That is, cut the cords which bind my feet, but under these circumstances, one does not look for style.)

"There is a knife somewhere—cut my feet! Cut my feet! Cut—cut—cut—" and at every "cut," Hicks, in his efforts to rise, rubs his face against the boards.

She remembers the voice; it is the English Manager. Has this scene been the result of some plot of his contriving? She does not pause to argue the question but hunts eagerly for the knife. After a hurried search she finds it, and hacks away at the strips which bind the wrists and ankles of the unhappy "Manager" alias "Ex-Bank Director."

At length his feet and hands are free; he rises heavily, and finds himself confronted by this beautiful girl, whose hair sweeps in waves, over her breast and shoulders.

"What does this mean?" she cries—her eyes wild with terror.

Stupified by the smoke and heat, Hicks cannot answer, he can only stare at the pale face of Kate, which every other moment is reddened by flashes of light. She seizes him, and shakes him by the arm—"Is there no way of escape? Must we be burned alive?"

He tears himself from her, and rushes to the window, but the smoke and flame drives him back. To the door, uttering horrible cries, but the door is locked, and he only hurts his feet by kicking the thick panels. And then, utterly overcome—scorched by heat and choked by smoke—Hicks falls upon the floor and lays there, like a bundle of "forgotten goods."

Poor Kate! Scarce knowing what to make of all this, she stands there, with the crimson light upon her face, and in the folds of her waving hair—she presses her hands to her bosom as she gasps for breath—she is conscious that she cannot live, in that horrible place, but a few moments longer.

With toil and poverty life is sweet to her; and she is struggling for it now, with every gasp of her hard-drawn breath.

But hark! Heavy steps upon the stair—a heavier sound against the door—it yields—and falls upon the body of the miserable Hicks. But what horrible apparition appears in the doorway?

Kate screams with terror; it is the Negro, who placed his hand to her mouth—he stands there, black and hideous, his white eyeballs rolling in his jetty face.

"Dey burn dis darkey alive? Yah—hah! Guess not! Dis darkey good for to stan' fire. Say! You dar Missus?"

And with a bound he is at her side—his brawny arm is about her waist.

"Come now! Don't you kick and scream—up stairs is de garret—tote along, Missus!"

With these words he bears her from the room, up the narrow stairs; up a narrower stairway, and then from a trap door, out upon a roof in flames.

Bulgine instinctively determines to save her—but when he finds himself on the hot roof, surrounded by flames—he gives up all for lost, and howling upon the Mob, who yell below, prepares to dash her down, and at the same time beat his brains out, against the pavement.

PART XX. THE POPLAR BOX.

When Elijah left his father, bound and helpless in the upper room of the den kept by the Bulgine, he made the best of his way into the heart of the city. Hurrying from the scene of the riot, he soon approached the house which, for a month or more, had been quietly occupied by Mr. Jacob D. Z. Hicks. It was an old three story brick, with its gable fronting on the street, from which it was separated by a small yard. Elijah's blood was in a tumult as he opened the gate and approached the door. The shutters of the house were closed from cellar to garret, and it was cast into shadow by the neighboring mansions.

"Now, we'll see whether the old man lied or not," said Elijah, as he opened the door with the key furnished him by Mr. Hicks.

He entered the house. All was desolate and still. He made his way straight to the room designated by his father, where stood the iron safe containing all the wealth of the old man. This room was on the third story, and in the back part of the house. Elijah ascended the stairs, and was astonished to find a lighted lamp placed on the floor of the entry in the third story. The door of the back room was opened, and a sound like the rustling of papers struck on his ear.

"Who can it be?" the thought flashed over him. He quietly took off his boots, and, passing the lamp, approached the door and looked within.

A man was standing near an iron safe, on which a lamp was placed. His back was toward Elijah, and he was engaged in examining the papers which he had taken from the safe. On a chair by his side was scattered a mass of gold and silver, mingled with bank notes.

"At last I've found the old scoundrel's Ark"—said the man, by way of soliloquy, and Elijah recognized the voice of Don Jorge. It was Don Jorge, attired in the guise of a Killer. Elijah stood in a position which enabled him to watch all the movements of the Cuban, without being himself observed; and Elijah's heart beat quick and his eyes glistened at the sight of the money which laid on the chair.

"I'll let him rob the chest,"—such was his thought, "and as he comes out of the room I'll force him to surrender."

At this moment he caught a side-view of the Cuban's face. It was stamped with a look of ineffable triumph, which displayed his white teeth under his dark mustache, and gave fresh brilliancy to his dark eyes.

"The money is good enough," he soliloquised, "these thousands will enable me to keep afloat for a year, at least, in Paris, or in some other continental city. As for the Cuban speculation, undertaken by some of my hot-headed compatriots—it's a humbug, and I'll have nothing more to do with it. They talk of love for their native land. Pshaw! Give me money, and I'll make my native land wherever wine and women are to be bought or sold."

With this remark he took the light from the top of the safe, and, sinking on his knees, he began to examine the interior. "There is a particular box which I must have"—he exclaimed—"It contains all the transactions between my father and Hicks—for that matter, between my father and more than five merchants of this good city, who have made fortunes by the slave trade. When I have the box in my hands I will hold a rod over their heads—"

Peering into the safe, he presently drew forth the object of his search—a box of unpainted poplar, not more than a foot long and six inches deep, which opened with a sliding lid.

"I can see no lock, and yet this slide is difficult to draw. Ah! It gives way—"

He began to draw the lid, which moved slowly as he passed his thumb in the crevice at one end, at the same time holding the box tightly against his breast.

Elijah was watching him all the while—panting for breath, and sinking his nails into the frame of the door, as he endeavored to subdue his excitement.

"Now we shall read the transactions of Captain Velasquez and Mr. Jacob Hicks," exclaimed Don Jorge—and it was the last word he ever spoke. The report of a pistol was heard. He sank backward on the floor, the box scattered into fragments over the room, while the lamp was momentarily obscured, by a veil of blueish smoke.

Elijah, stupified by the sudden report, rushed into the room, and took hold of the prostrate man. His face was blue with the death agony. Once his lips moved—his eyes rolled in their sockets—and then his lips were motionless and his eyes fixed in death. The blood oozed slowly from a wound near his heart. His knees bent, and his legs doubled under him, he lay dead upon the floor, his arms thrown out, on either hand, the fingers stiff and cramped.

Mr. Hicks for reasons of his own, had concealed a loaded pistol in the poplar box, which was connected with the sliding lid, by a complication of clock work machinery. The pistol was so arranged that the drawing of the lid pulled the trigger. And the lid could not be drawn, unless the box was placed against the breast, in such a manner, that the muzzle of the concealed pistol, would rest within ten inches of the heart of the man, who might attempt to open it.

Don Jorge had drawn the sliding lid, and paid for that trifling deed with his life.

He lay dead upon the floor; as dead indeed, as any Negro that he had ever pitched from the deck of his Slaver, in the midst of the broad Ocean.

Elijah wasted no time in useless efforts to restore the dead man to life. Gathering up the gold and silver, which laid upon the chair, he poured it into his pockets, together with a goodly store of bank notes. Then without a word, he quietly left the room, and descended the stairs. Before five minutes were gone, he had left the house, carefully locking the front door behind him.

"The old man did not lie—there was money there," he soliloquized, as he hurried back to the scene of the Riot," "wonder if he intended that box for me?"

He lost no time, but made the best of his way toward the Den of the Bulgine, and approached it by the alley, which communicated with the back door. Emerging from the darkness of the alley, he heard at once the roar of the mob, and the roar of the flames. The yard was deserted. The flames ascended from the shed to the roof. Elijah heard the shout of the multitude, who were packed together in front of the house, in Dog Alley, and at once remembered the condition in which he had left his father. How should he save him? Jumping upon the fence, he saw at a glance that he might ascend to the roof of the next house, (which was deserted) by placing a board upon the shed which rose from the ground to its second story window. It was the work of a few moments to tear a board from the fence—climb upon the shed, drawing the board after him—and then rest one end of the board upon the shed, while the other reached the edge of the low roof. Crawling cat-like on hands and knees, Elijah began the ascent.

Half-way up, the board began to slip, but Elijah kept on, and mounted the roof, at the same moment that the board fell beneath him. Once on the roof, he ascended to the ridge, and saw at the first glance, a sight which quickened his blood. The faces of the mob—the Den of the Bulgine in flames—and the Bulgine himself standing black and gigantic, in the centre of the flames—standing upon the roof, and near the very edge—with the body of a woman in his arms.

"It's Kate!" cried Elijah, and with an incoherent yell, he sprang upon the burning roof. The multitude beheld him, and answered his yell with shouts of horror and ejaculations of feverish suspense. They saw him wrapped in smoke and flame, and in an instant, saw him emerge from the cloud and reach the Negro's side. And then the shouts of the spectators, as they beheld the figures on the roof, now revealed in light, and now lost in smoke, ascended tumultuously upon the air.

"The nigger won't give him the gal!" cried one.

"They're fightin!" shouted another.

"It's 'Lije—hurry and pitch him over!" was the address of one of the most prominent among the Killers.

But the Bulgine, Elijah and the insensible girl were lost to view in the thick cloud which swept over the roof of the burning house. The suspense of the spectators did not long continue. A dull, deafening crash was heard—"the roof has fallen in!" rang from a thousand throats, and for a while the blackness of mid-night descended upon the scene. Then, up from the house, and through the thick blackness which covered it, shot a column of blazing cinders, brightening up once more the faces of the spectators, and throwing a livid glare into the heavens.

[161]

By that light, the riot began once more. The Bulgine, the girl and the convict had been engulfed in the flames; and the Killers and their confederate rioters seeing nothing especial to occupy their attention, now that the crisis of the scene was over, went to work again, and carried the 'terror of their arms' into the heart of the 'negro camp.' How they rioted at intervals through the whole night—how by morning-light the military came hurrying to the scene, their duty being to make up by ball and buckshot for the cowardice and misconduct of the civil authorities—all this may be read in the daily papers of October 1849.[37]

The second day after the riot, two bodies were found in the cellar of the burnt hovel, their charred features, covered by wet and smouldering embers. Which was the body of Bulgine, and which the body of Mr. Jacob D. Z. Hicks, none of the spectators could tell; an old woman who stood in the midst of the assembled throng declared that one of the bodies, was that of her son, Elijah Watson.

"But my child—poor Kate, my child! Where's her body gone to? Can't nobody tell? What was she doin' in that nigger's hut, when it was set afire? Can't nobody tell?"

In vain did Mrs. Watson utter these questions with all the emphasis of her shrill voice. Nobody could tell, except indeed the old lady herself, and she wisely held her peace.

Further search into the smouldering embers disclosed the remains of another body, so horribly burnt and disfigured as to be utterly undistinguishable. Was it the body of Cromwell, Elijah, or Kate?

PART XXI. CONCLUSION.

In the Trials of the Rioters, which took place within a month after the Riots, no one will be able to discover the name of Elijah Watson. Nor has Kate ever been seen, since the night of the Riots, among the supernumeraries of the theatre. Whatever became of them—whether they escaped from the burning roof, just before it fell, or whether they were engulfed in the ruins—cannot be distinctly stated. One incident will bring this narrative to a close. A Philadelphia merchant, who had been connected with Mr. Hicks in his palmiest days, was observed to be in a great tremor, soon after the riots. He had become aware of the *suicide* of Don Jorge in the house of Mr. Hicks; in fact, he had visited that house, the day after the riot, seeking Mr. Hicks on business connected with the *African* trade, and had found only the dead body of Don Jorge. Our merchant did not waste much time in the house, but hurried away to his own residence, where he was confronted by a young lady, who spake of matters which drove the very life-blood from his cheek.

The young lady—to the merchant unknown—had in some manner come into possession of those papers of the deceased Hicks, which implicated some four or five respectable houses in the profitable transactions of the African Slave Trade. Our merchant was among the number.

And in a clear voice the young woman demanded a certain favor as the price of her secrecy. She was not to be frightened; the goodly man of business tried in vain to terrify her with the threat of a prosecution for "Conspiracy to extort money." She replied by stating every little fact embraced in the papers aforesaid, copies of which she placed in the hands of the respectable man. And he grew paler and trembled more violently as she continued her narrative. She was a very beautiful, and yet a very determined young woman.

He took counsel with *the other parties* implicated, and agreed to grant her request.*

This request granted, the young lady disappeared, and was not again heard from, until the commencement of December, when our Merchant and his confederates—all Respectable Killers—received a large pacquet, which had been brought from Chagres by the steamer Empire City. It was dated "PANAMA, *Nov. 2nd*, 1849—and contained all the documents about the slave trade, together with the following letter, which we transcribe, and which brings this Narrative to a close.

PANAMA, Nov. 2, 1849.

To —— Esq., Philadelphia.

SIR:—You and your friends have fulfilled your promise, to secure for Elijah and myself an unmolested departure from your city, and a safe passage to Panama. And I now fulfil mine by transmitting to you the accompanying

---

* As a note to the above we append the following paragraph, which we extract from the Message of President Taylor transmitted to Congress, on the 24th of December, 1849.[38]

"Your attention is earnestly invited to an amendment of our existing laws relating to the African slave trade, with a view to the effectual suppression of that barbarous traffic. It is not to be denied, that this trade is still, in part, carried on by means of vessels built in the United States, and owned or navigated by some of our citizens. The correspondence between the Department of State and the Minister and Consul of the United States at Rio de Janeiro, which has from time to time been laid before Congress, represents that it is a customary device to evade the penalties of our laws by means of sea letters. Vessels sold in

papers which you will understand. Elijah and myself start for San Francisco to-morrow, where some day or other we may be heard from by other names, and under better circumstances than those which surrounded us in Philadelphia.

Yours, &c.,

KATE WATSON.

THE END.

Brazil, when provided with such papers by the Consul, instead of returning to the United States for a new register, proceed, at once, to the coast of Africa, for the purpose of obtaining cargoes of slaves. Much additional information of the same character, has recently been transmitted to the Department of State."

APPENDIX 1

Life and Adventures of Charles Anderson Chester

" A cry at once arose that a white man was shot, and the attention of the mob was directed to the California House, at th corner of Sixth and St. Mary street."—page 30

FIGURE 8. "A cry at once arose that a white man was shot."

George Lippard, *Life and Adventures of Charles Anderson Chester*
(Philadelphia: Yates and Smith, 1849/50), frontispiece. Am 1850 Lif 76423.O.
Courtesy of the Library Company of Philadelphia.

(facing page)
FIGURE 9. Title page.

George Lippard, *Life and Adventures of Charles Anderson Chester*
(Philadelphia: Yates and Smith, 1849/50). Am 1850 Lif 76423.O.
Courtesy of the Library Company of Philadelphia.

LIFE AND ADVENTURES

OF

CHARLES ANDERSON CHESTER,

THE

NOTORIOUS LEADER OF THE

PHILADELPHIA "KILLERS."

WHO WAS MURDERED, WHILE ENGAGED IN THE DESTRUCTION
OF THE CALIFORNIA HOUSE, ON ELECTION NIGHT,
OCTOBER 11, 1849.

Taken from a daguerreotype, previous to Chester's going to Havana.

PRINTED FOR THE PUBLISHERS.
PHILADELPHIA.
1850.

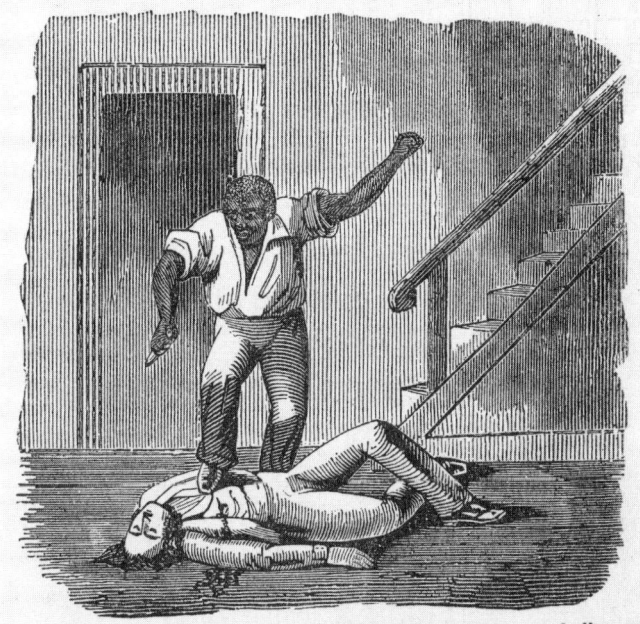

"Come on you dam Killers," he bawled, "I've stuck your bully, and I'm ready for de wust of you!"—page 34.

FIGURE 10. "Charles Anderson Chester Murdered by Black Herkles."

George Lippard, *Life and Adventures of Charles Anderson Chester* (Philadelphia: Yates and Smith, 1849/50), p. 9. Am 1850 Lif 76423.O. Courtesy of the Library Company of Philadelphia.

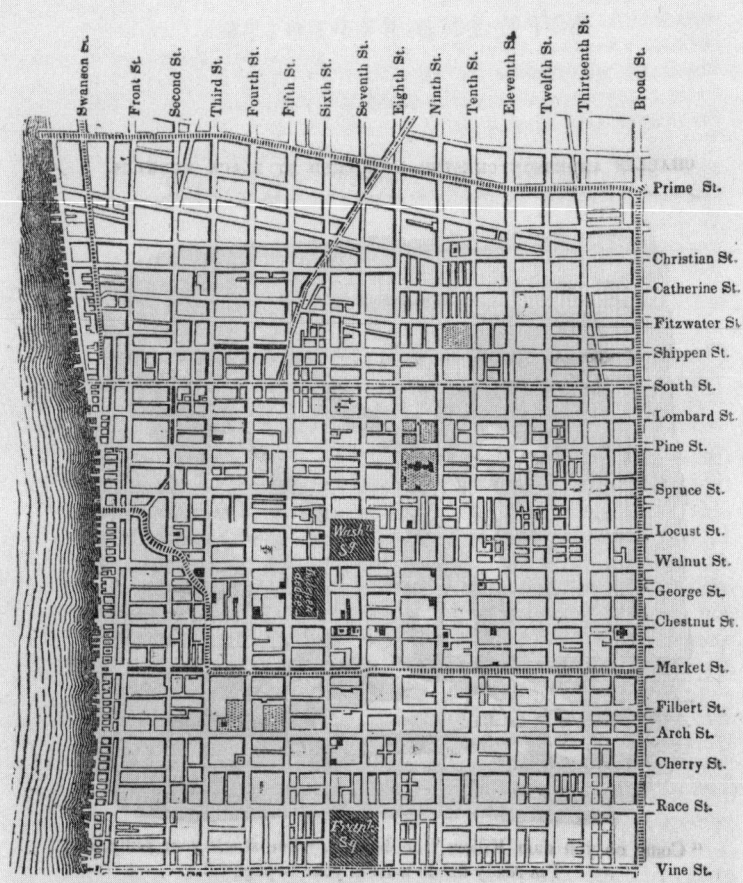

MAP of the City and Districts of Moyamensing and Southwark, from the river
Delaware to Broad street,

† ↓ The scene of Riot at Sixth and St. Mary streets.

FIGURE 11. "MAP of the City and Districts of Moyamensing and
Southwark." The map appears here as originally printed, its orientation
inverted from the customary one, with north at the bottom.

George Lippard, *Life and Adventures of Charles Anderson Chester*
(Philadelphia: Yates and Smith, 1849/50), p. 10. Am 1850 Lif 76423.O.
Courtesy of the Library Company of Philadelphia.

THE

LIFE AND EXPLOITS

OF

CHARLES ANDERSON CHESTER.

CHAPTER I.

*Charles Anderson Chester—His youth and parentage—Adventures
at College—Letter from his Father—Flight from College.*

Charles Anderson Chester, the subject of this eventful
narrative, was the son of a wealthy, and as the world goes, a respectable parentage. His father was at once a Merchant and a Banker;
and his mother was the daughter of a millionaire. Accustomed
from his earliest years to all that wealth can offer, to pamper the
appetite and deprave the passions, Anderson grew to manhood
with a great sense of his own importance derived from the wealth
of his father. He was sent at the age of eighteen, from the roof of his
father's splendid mansion, to a New England College, "to complete
his education." His education supposed to have been commenced
at the University of Pennsylvania, had in reality begun at the Hunt-
ing Park Race Course, at the Chesnut Street gambling hell, the
Theatre and the Brothel. At eighteen he was already known as a
"man about town." He drove the handsomest turn out on Broad
Street; he played "Brag,"[1] with the oldest gamesters, and drank his

four bottles of Champaigne with the most experienced of veteran drunkards. And thus initiated into life, he went to New England to finish his education.

Here his career was short and brilliant. He flogged his tutor, attempted to set fire to the College buildings and was very nearly successful in an attempt to abduct the only daughter of the President. These, with numerous minor exploits produced his expulsion after a brief period of six months.

At this state of affairs Anderson knew not what to do. He did not like the idea of returning home. His father was a bon vivant,—a good liver of the canvass back order,—liberal at times,—but again as obstinate as the pride of money, and the habit of commanding men's lives with the power of money, could make him. He was withal a nominal member of a wealthy Church. He might possibly wink at Anderson's Collegiate exploits, and term them the effusions of a "spirited nature" winding up with a check for a $1000, or he might bid his son to go to sea, to list in the army, or go to a place not mentioned to ears polite. What would be his course? Anderson could not tell.

He was sitting in his room, at the crack hotel of the College town, when he received his father's letter. He had spent his last dollar. He was in arrears for board. He was beset by duns, duns of every shape from the waiter to the washer-woman. While meditating over the state of affairs he received his father's letter. It was terse and to the point.

SIR:—You have made your bed and you must lie down in it. Expect nothing from me. You can choose your own course. At the same time, you will distinctly understand, that by your conduct you have cast off all claims upon your family, who desire to hear nothing from you until you are sincerly repentent for the disgrace which your behaviour has heaped upon them.

JACOB CHESTER.

This was not a very fatherly letter it must be confessed, though the conduct of Anderson had been bad enough. He read it over and over again—held it near the light until the glare played over his face, corrugated by silent rage,—and after a few moments consigned it to his vest pocket.

All was still in the hotel. He at once determined upon his plan. Dressing himself in a green walking coat trimmed with metal buttons, plaid pants and buff vest, Anderson walked quietly from his room, and as quietly left the hotel at the dead hour of the night. He left without "bag or baggage," and striking over the fields, through a driving mist, he made his way to a railway station distant some five miles. The passions of a demon were working in his heart, for the manner in which his father had winked at his early faults, only served to render his letter more intolerable and galling.

How he obtained passage in the cars we cannot tell. Suffice it to say, that after two days he landed in Philadelphia, his apparel dusty and way-worn, and his shirt collar hidden ominously behind the folds of his black cravat.

He was tall for his age. His chin already was darkened by a beard that would not have shamed a Turk. Light complexioned and fair haired, he was the very figure to strike the eye on Chesnut street, or amid the buz and uproar of a ball.

Dusty, tired and hungry, he made the best of his way to his father's mansion. He was determined to have an interview with the old man. Stepping up the marble stair case, he rung the bell, and stood for a few moments with a fluttering heart. A strange servant answered the bell, and greeted him with the news, "that Mr. Chester and his family had left for Cape May the week before."

This was bad news for Anderson. Turning from his father's house, he sauntered listlessly toward the Exchange,[2] until he came near his father's store,—a dark old brick building, standing sullen and gloomy amid fashionable dwellings of modern construction. He entered the counting room. It was situated at the farther end of a large gloomy place, and was fenced off from bales of goods, and hogsheads of cogniac, by a dingy railing of unpainted pine.

CHAPTER II.

Mr. Smick the head clerk—The check for $5,000—Charles contrives a scheme—Its result—Interview with a certain personage which has an important bearing on his fate—The British Captain.

"Where is Mr. Smick?" asked Anderson of the negro porter, who was the only person visible.

"Jist gone out," answered the porter, who did not recognize his employer's son, "Back d'rectly.

"I'll wait for him," was the answer, and Anderson sauntered into the counting room, which was furnished with an old chair, a large desk and range of shelves filled with ledgers, etc.

An opened letter, spread upon the desk, attracted the eye of the hopeful youth. It was from Cape May, bore the signature of his father, was addressed to Mr. Smick his head clerk, and contained this brief injunction.—[3]

"Smick—I send you a check for $5,000. Cash it, and meet that note of Johns & Brother—to-morrow—you understand."

"Where the deuce is the check?" soliloquized Anderson, and forthwith began to search for it, but in vain. While thus engaged his ear was attracted by the sound of a footstep. Looking through the railing he beheld a short little man with a round face and a hooked nose, approaching at a brisk pace. As he saw him, his fertile mind, hit upon a plan of operations.

"Smick my good fellow," he said as the head clerk opened the door of the counting-room—"I've been looking for you all over town. Quick! At Walnut street wharf! There's no time to be lost!"

He spoke these incoherent words with every manifestation of alarm and terror. As much surprised at the sudden appearance of the vagabond son in the counting room, as at his hurried words, the head clerk was for a few moments at a loss for words.

"You here—umph! Thought you was at college—eh!" exclaimed Smick as soon as he found his tongue—"Walnut street wharf! What *do* you mean?"

"Mr. Smick," responded the young man slowly and with deliberation, "I mean that on returning from Cape May father has been stricken with an apopletic fit. He's on board of the boat. Mother sent me up here, to tell you to come down without delay. Quick! No time's to be lost."

Smick seemed thunderstricken. He placed his finger on the tip of his nose, muttering "Chester struck with apoplexy—bad, bad! Here's this check to be cashed, and that note of Johns & Brother to be met. What shall I do—"

"I'll tell you Smick. Give me the check—I'll get it cashed and then go and take up the note, while you hurry down to the wharf."

He said this in quite a confidential manner, laying his hand on Smick's arm and looking very knowingly into his face.

In answer to this, Mr. Smick closed one eye—arranged his white cravat—and seemed buried in thought, while Charles stood waiting with evident impatience for his answer.

"You've been to Cape May—have you?" he said, regarding Charles with one eye closed.

"You know I have not. I have just got on from New York, and met one of father's servants, as I was coming off the boat. He told me the old gentleman had been taken with apoplexy on the way up. I went into the cabin of the Cape May boat which had just come to, and saw father there. Mother gave me the message which I have just delivered. Indeed, Mr. Smick you'd better hurry."

"Then you had better take the check," said Smick extending his hand. "Get it cashed and take up that note. It is now half past two, it must be done without delay."

His eyes glistening Charles reached forth his hand to grasp the check, when Mr. Smick drew back his hand, quietly observing at the same time "I think Charles you had better ask your father. Here he is. Rather singular that he's so soon recovered from his fit of apoplexy!"

Scarcely had the words passed his lips, when at his shoulder, appeared the portly figure of the father,—Mr. Jacob Chester, a gentleman of some fifty years, dressed in black with a white waist-coat. His ruddy face was overspread with a scowl; he regarded his son with a glance full of meaning, at the same time passing his kerchief incessantly over his bald crown. He had overheard the whole of the conversation between his son and his head clerk. He had indeed returned from Cape May, but had seen his clerk, *only five minutes previous to this interview*. His feelings as he overheard the conversation may be imagined.

"Scoundrel!" was his solitary ejaculation, as he gazed upon his son, who now stood cowering and abashed, in one corner of the counting room.

"Father—" hesitated Charles.

The merchant pointed to the door.

"Go!" he said, and motioned with his finger.

"Forgive me father,—I've been wild. I know it," faltered Charles.

"You saw me in a fit, did you? And you would have got that check cashed and taken up Johns' note, would you? You're a bigger scoundrel than I took you for. Go!"

Charles moved to the door. While Smick stood thunderstricken, the father followed his son into the large room, which, filled with hogsheads and bales, intervened between the counting-room and the street. Charles quietly threaded his way through the gloomy place, and was passing to the street when his father's hand stopped him on the threshold.

"Charles," said he, "let us understand one another."

Charles turned with surprise pictured on his face; the countenance of his father was fraught with a meaning which he could not analyze.

"In the first place," said the Merchant, "read this."

He handed his son a copy of the New York Herald, dated the day previous. The finger of Mr. Jacob Chester pointed a paragraph embodied in a letter from Cape May. Charles read in silence, his face displaying every change of incredulity succeeded by surprise. Thus read the paragraph:

"By the by you have heard that a distinguished scion of the British aristocracy, who passes under the title of the Hon. Capt. Fritz-Adam, has been figuring rather extensively at this place. The Captain is a gallant gentleman, with a pale mouse coloured moustache and aristocratic air. He has excited quite a sensation. He is altogether a man of ton—elegant and fascinating; so much so, that yesterday the young wife of one of our old Philadelphia merchants was detected in a rather embarrassing situation, with the gallant Briton, and worst of all, the discoverer was her venerable spouse. The affair has created a great talk. To-morrow I will send you full particulars."

"Well, what of this?" said Charles looking into his father's face.

"Nothing much. Only that young wife of an old merchant, was your mother. I married her at sixteen; married her out of regard for her family, and have lived with her these nineteen years. She is now about thirty-five, but as young and lively as ever. The day before yesterday she disgraced me at Cape May, and strengthened a resolve which I have long indulged, to wit, to cast her and her son to the winds, or to the d—l. You comprehend Charles? You are not my son. The conduct of your mother breaks all ties between us. For nineteen years I have supported you. You can gamble, drink, and act the gentleman in every way. Your education is complete. My advice to you, is, to follow you[4] mother, who yesterday eloped with her British Captain. From me, from this hour, you can expect nothing. Beg, starve, or steal, as you please, do it in a gentlemanly way if you like, but from me you shall never receive one cent. We understand one another. Good day, sir."

With these words the old man turned away, leaving Charles pale and thunderstricken on the threshhold. The thunderbolt which had fallen upon him, deprived him for the time of all control over his reason. He was stupefied

CHAPTER III.

Mr. Joe Bright and the letters—A peep into important correspondence—Mr. Wilmins the Broker—Drafts for $5060— New York and Havana.

At last, still holding the New York Herald in his hand, he took his way from Mr. Jacob Chester's store. As he passed along the street, he tried, for a long time without success, to realize his situation. His mother a disgraced woman—himself pronounced an illegitimate by the man whom he had always known as his father— he could not believe it. But the New York Herald was in his hands, the words of the old Merchant still rang in his ears. Then when he contrasted the youth of his mother with the age of her husband, her fondness for admiration and show with the painstaking habits of the merchant, the story appeared more reasonable. A thousand things came to the memory of Charles, which served to confirm the story of Mr. Jacob Chester. Suffice it to say that after an hour's walk up one street and down another, Charles found himself at the corner of Fourth and Walnut street with three facts impressed rather vividly upon his mind. He was without a father; his mother had eloped with a mustache (appended to a British Captain) and he, Charles Anderson Chester, was without a cent in the world.

Charles surveyed his apparel. Green coat, plaid pants and buff vest looked remarkably seedy. He felt his pocket.[5] They were deplorably empty. He looked up and down Walnut street, as night began to gather over the town, and brought himself to the conclusion, expressed in these words, muttered through his set teeth— "Without father or mother, friend or dollar, my chance of a bed and supper to night gets dim and dimmer."

In this mood he took his way toward the Exchange. He was roused from a reverie by a hand laid on his arm, and by the words, "How d'ye do, Mister Charles."

Starting from his gloomy reverie, Charles beheld a youth of some fourteen years, whose snub nose and red hair, together with nankeen pants and cassimere jacket, brought home to him the fact, that he beheld no less a personage than Mr. Joe. Bright, who was employed in a double capacity,—half as errand boy and half as under clerk—in his father's store. Joe was delighted to see Mr. Charles,—asked him when he had arrived in the city—how long he intended to stay, et cetera. As for Charles quietly keeping his eye upon the youth, who held a package in his right hand, he said:

"Give me the letters Joe. I'll take them up to the house. As for you, father wants you to go up to the Baltimore Rail Road Depot, and bring down a box that is there, addressed to him. Just tell the Agent that father sent you, and he'll give you the box. Mind that you hurry back."

Without a word the red haired youth handed the letters to Mr. Charles, and hurried up Walnut street, on his way to Eleventh & Market. Charles slipped the letters into his pocket, gazed for a moment after the form of the errand boy, and then hurrying down Walnut street, turned into a "pot house" whose sign displayed tempting inducements to "sailors and emigrants." It was a miserable place, with one chair, a bar, and a little man, with a dirty face and one eye.

"What'll yez plase to have, Sur?"

Charles called for a glass of whiskey, and turning his back to the landlord, drew the package from his pocket and proceeded to count the letters which he had received from Joe. There were ten in all; one was particularly heavy; and all of them were carefully sealed. Did one, or did all of them contain money? This was an important question, but Charles did not choose to solve it in the pot house. But how shall he pay for his glass of whiskey? He had not a penny in the world. This placed him in a decidedly bad predicament. Waiting until the landlord had turned his back, for a moment, Charles passed quietly from the place, and hurried up Walnut street, turned into Dock, and in a few moments was in Third street in the vicinity of Chesnut.

He had decided upon a difficult step. The letters which he held, bore the postmarks of distant parts of the Union, and very possibly they contained drafts upon houses in New York.

It was his resolution to ascertain the fact in the first place and in the second to get these drafts cashed. It was after bank hours, and only two broker's offices in the vicinity remained open. Charle's[6] brain was in a whirl; conscious that whatever he did must be done without delay, he stood on the sidewalk, with his finger raised to his forehead, anxiously engaged in cogitating some scheme, which might enable him to cash the drafts in the letters,—that is, if said letters happened to contain drafts, or money in any shape.

But was this the case? Charles turned into an alley and with a trembling hand broke the seals of the letters. His brain reeled as thier[7] contents were disclosed to his gloating eyes. For those letters did contain drafts at one two and three days sight, drawn upon certain firms in New York, and amounting altogether to five thousand and sixty dollars. Crumpling the letters drafts and all into his pocket, Charles staggered from the alley like a drunken man. He had resolved upon his course of action. Entering a small periodical agency, he called for pen and paper, and (while the boy in attendance was waiting upon a customer) our hero, proceeded in quite a business like manner to sign the name of "Jacob Chester" upon each of those talismanic slips of paper. Habit had made him familiar with his late father's signature; he wrote with ease and facility; in a few moments the work was done. He carefully sanded the signatures, and then made the best of his way to the office of a celebrated Broker, with whom his father had dealt for many years. On the threshold he paused; his heart beat like the pendulum of a clock; gazing through the glass door he beheld the familiar face of the Broker, bald-head, high shirt collar, gold spectacles and all. For a moment the young gentleman hesitated; at length commanding all the force of his nerves he entered, and spreading the magic slips of paper upon the counter, said with great self-possession, "Mister Wilmins, father starts for Niagara early in the morning. He would take it as a favour, if you would cash these drafts to-night."

The Broker recognized Charles, addressed him by name, and after a word or two as to his father's health, examined the drafts, first one side and then the other. This done, he paused, and surveyed Charles through his gold spectacles. Charles never forgot that scrutinizing gaze. "He suspects something," he muttered to himself, while, in fact, the worthy Broker, who was somewhat absent-minded, was cogitating whether or no he should ask Charles as to the truth of that story about the British Captain.

"Five thousand and sixty dollars," said the Broker.

"Can you do it?" gasped Charles, much agitated, but endeavouring to look as calm as possible.

"Certainly," was the answer. "Would your father like city or New York funds?"

"As you please," faltered Charles, "only he wanted a thousand in twenties."

The Broker unlocked his iron-safe and counted out five thousand and sixty dollars; forty $100 bills, and the balance in $20 notes; Charles watching him all the while with a feverish eye.

Charles extended his hand, and could scarce believe the evidence of his senses, when he felt the silken slips of paper between his fingers. He thrust them into his breast pocket, and hurried to the door.

"Ah! come back, young man," he heard the voice of the Broker.

It was the first impulse of Charles to put to his heels, but turning with a pallid face, he again confronted the spectacled Broker.

"Young man—that is, Mr. Chester," began the Broker, "If its not impolite I'd like to ask you one question."

Charles shook in "his boots," but managed to falter out the monosyllable, "Well?"

"Is there any truth in that story—eh, eh—about the Brit— British Captain—and—" he paused.

Charles raised his handkerchief to his eye, and in a voice broken by emotion, faltered—

"Too true! Alas! It is too true!" and as if overcome by his feeling hastened from the Broker's store.

Making the best of his way down Third, he struck into Dock street, and then turned down Walnut street. As he approached the corner of Front and Walnut street, he heard the ring of a bell. Utterly bewildered by the incidents of the last hour, he was hurrying at random,—he knew not whither—when the ringing of the bell decided him, as to his future course.

"It's the New York bell!" he muttered, and in five minutes had purchased his ticket, and was on board the steamboat, on his way to New York.

That night at ten he landed at the foot of Courtlandt street. Without pausing to eat or sleep, he proceeded to a barber shop and had his face cleanly shaved. Then, in an hour's ramble he provided himself with a large trunk, a black wig, a pair of false whiskers, and two suits of clothes. He assumed the wig and whiskers in the street; put on a single breasted frock coat, buttoning to the neck, in a tailor's store; covered his forehead with a glazed cap, and then calling a hack directed the driver to take his trunk to Bloodgood's Hotel.[8]

He entered his name on the books in this style, "ALFRED DU-FRENAY, CHICAGO."

His next care was to look at the New York Sun of that date. The shipping advertisements first arrested his attention. One in especial rivetted his eye. He perused it attentively, and presently sallied from the Hotel, called a cab, and directed the driver to carry him, in "double quick time," to the Battery. Arrived at this point, he took a boat, and rowed out into the stream, and was presently on board of a steamer which lay at anchor in the bay. He saw the Captain, paid his fare, despatched a messenger for his trunks, and before morning was fifty miles beyond Sandy Hook on his way to Havana.

On the second day of her passage the steamer spoke a vessel bound for Philadelphia. Letters were exchanged, and Charles took this opportunity to send the following to his late father:

VENERABLE SIR:—You told me to follow my mother. I am after her.

Your obedient son,

CHARLES ANDERSON CHESTER.

P. S.—Hope those drafts came to hand?

This letter reached his father, at the very moment, when he was sitting over his wine, engaged in conversation with the Broker, who was calmly endeavouring to convince him, that certain drafts which he held, bore the signature of "JACOB CHESTER."

And here, while the son is on his way to Havana, and the father and the Broker are talking together, we will leave our characters, while two years pass away. These events occurred in 1846; it is 1849 when we again resume our story. Between these years Mr. Jacob Chester failed, and it was rumoured in Philadelphia, in the summer of 1849, that his son had returned to that city, in disguise, on business connected with the celebrated Cubian[9] expedition.

CHAPTER IV.

*Ophelia Thompson—The "Supernumary"[10]—How she was
followed and what was the result.*

IN the month of October 1849, a young woman, who was connected with one of the Theatres in a subordinate capacity, excited considerable attention, on the part of those gentlemen who prowl about the stage seeking "whom they may devour." We allude to that class of persons, young and old, who insult respectable women

[187]

in the street, parade opera glasses in the pit, while the dancing is in progress, and hang around the green room, where the actors congregate when their presence is not needed upon the stage.

This young woman was altogether a subordinate; she did not appear in any leading character, but was seen as an assistant in the ballet; or as a part of some dramatic spectacle; in fact, she was what is generally denominated "a supernumary." She was about eighteen years of age; rather tall, was known by the name of Ophelia Thompson; with brown hair, dark eyes, a noble bust, and a walk that would not have disgraced an empress. She was new to the stage. Who or what she was, no one knew; not even the manager who paid her 37½ cents per night, for her services in the *ballet* and spectacle. She had only been engaged a week, in October 1849, when her beauty made considerable buz among the libertines of the pit, and the loungers of the green room. Her modest manner, and her evident desire to remain unobserved and unknown, only whetted the curiosity of these vultures who prey upon female beauty and innocence.

One night, however, as winding her faded shawl about her shoulders, and drawing her green veil over her face, she left the Theatre, on her way to her unknown home; she was followed,—at a discreet distance—by one of those gentlemen of the character named above. He was rather portly; wore a bangup which concealed the lower part of his face, and carried a large bone headed stick. The object of his pursuit led him a devious chase. Up one street and down another, now passing through narrow alleys, and now along the streets, she hurried on, until at last she reached a small frame house, which stood at the extremity of a dark court, in that district somewhat widely known as "Moyamensing." A lamp standing at the entrance of the court, emitted a faint and dismal light. When she reached the lamp she paused, and looked around her, as though she was conscious or afraid that she had been followed. The gentleman with the big stick saw her turn, and skulked behind a convenient corner, in time to avoid her observation. In a moment she resumed her way and entered the frame tenement, from the window of which, a faint light shone out upon the pavement. The portly gentlemen[11] stole cautiously to the window, took one glance and then crouched against the door of the house. That glance however, had revealed to him, a small room miserably furnished, with an old woman sitting near a smouldering fire, and a young one—"the supernumary" of the Theatre—standing by her side, one hand laid upon a pine table and the other raised as if in the act of expostulation.

The portly gentlemen did his best to overhear the conversation which took place between the two. Pressing his ear against a chink of the door, and balancing himself with his stick as he knelt on one knee, he managed to overhear a portion of the following conversation.

"So you've come,—have you?" said the old woman, in a voice between a grunt and a growl.

"Yes, mother. And there's my week's salary—just two dollars and a quarter."

"Two dollars and a quarter! And how's a-body as is old and has the rheumatiz, to live on two dollars and a quarter?"

"Mother I do all that I can, I'm sure. I'd earn more if I could."

"Bah! If you only know'd what's what, you might earn a heap I tell you. Here since your father's been dead,—killed by fallin' off a buildin' two years ago—I've had all the keer of you and tuk in

washin' when you was goin' to school. And now when you're grow'd
up and kin do somethin' for your mother, why you don't do it.

"What *can* I do mother?" said the young woman, in a voice
of entreaty.

The old woman replied with a sound between a cough and
a laugh as she said.

"What kin you do? Why if I was young and handsom' and
had a foot and a face like yourn,—and danced at the Theater, I'd
show you, what *I* could do. Ain't there plenty of rich gentlemen,
as 'ud be glad to pay you your weight in goold if—

The rest of the sentence was lost in a whisper, but the gentlemen in[12] the big stick who listened at the door, heard the reply of
the girl, which consisted in a simple ejaculation, uttered in a tone
of reproach and shame.

"My God, mother!"

"Yes, it is easy to say my God, *mother*!" replied the old woman
mimicking her daughter, "But if you only had the spunk of a lobster
you might roll in goold an' be a great actress an'—what not!"

The listener did not wait for another word, but pushing open
the door, entered the apartment. The old woman looked up in
surprise, her haggard face looking almost ghastly, by lamp light,
while the daughter (who had thrown her bonnet and shawl aside)
gazed upon the intruder in evident alarm.

"Don't mind me, my good friends, don't mind me," said the
portly gentleman, in a thick voice, as he approached the table;
"I'm a friend, that's all. Have seen your daughter on the stage, and
would like to make a great actress of her. Will take charge of her
tuition. That can't be managed without money, but money's no
object to me."

And stepping between the mother and daughter he laid five bright gold pieces upon the pine table.

"Here's luck!" screeched the old woman, grasping for the money.

"What say you?" asked the portly gentleman addressing the daughter.

"I—don't—know—you—sir—" she exclaimed with a proud curl of the lip, as her bosom swelled under its shabby covering. At the same time she wrenched the money from her mother's grasp. "Take your money, sir."

There was something queenly in the look of the young woman, as with her form swelling to its full stature, she regarded the intruder with a look of withering scorn, extending his gold pieces in one hand and at the same time pointing to the door.

"The very thing! That voice would do honor to Fanny Kemble! I tell you Miss that nature cut you out for an actress—a great actress."

"So nature' did," exclaimed the old woman, rising from her chair—"Take the money girl, and let this gentleman make a great actress of you."

"Either you must leave the house or I will," said the girl, and dashing the gold pieces into the face of the portly gentleman, she retreated behind the table, her eye flashing and her bosom swelling with anger. This action rather disconcerted the gentleman. Retreating backward, and bowing at the same time, he stumbled over the threshold, and gathered himself up, in time to receive the gold pieces in his face a second time, from the hand of the girl.

She had gathered them from the floor, in defiance of the objurgations of her mother, who earnestly sought to retain only a single piece.

CHAPTER V.

The old woman and Mr. Jacob Chester—It's a bargain.

"Now mother," said the girl closing the door, and placing her hand firmly on the old woman's shoulder, "if I hear, after this, one word from your lips, like those you have spoken to-night, we part forever."

Her flashing eye and deep-toned voice impressed the old woman with a sensation between rage and fear. But ere she could frame a reply, her daughter had gone up stairs, and the old woman heard a sound like the closing of a bolt.

"One of her tantrums. When things don't go right, she goes to bed without supper and locks herself in. Lor' how they brings up children now-a-days!"

For a long time she sat in silence, stretching her withered hands over the fire; at length she took the light and hobbling to the door unlocked it, and went out into the court. Bending down, the light extended in her skinny fingers and playing over her haggard face, she groped in the mud and filth for the gold pieces, which her daughter had flung into the face of the portly gentleman.

"*Won,*" she mumbled seizing a bright object which sparkled in the mud, when a hand touched her lightly on the arm, and looking up she saw the portly gentleman at her side.

He pointed to the door of the frame house, and led the way. She followed, and after closing the street door and the door which opened on the stairway, they sat down together and conversed for a long time in whispers, the old woman's face manifesting a feverish lust for gain, while the portly gentleman suffered his coat collar to fall on his shoulders, until his face was visible. He next removed his hat. It was the face of Mr. Jacob Chester, bald-head, white cravat and all,—a little older than when we last beheld him—yet with a bright twinkle in his eyes, and a sort of amorous grin upon his lips. They conversed for a long time and the termination of the conversation was in these words:—

"To-morrow night as she is going to the theatre," said Mr. Jacob—"It is election night and the streets will be full of bonfires and devilment. She can be seized at the corner of the street, put into a cab which I have ready, and kept quiet until her temper is a little managable."

He laid some bank notes and bright gold pieces upon the table, which the old woman seized with a hungry grasp as she replied:—

"Yes, and Black Herkles is the man to do it. Have everything ready, and it kin be done. You'd better see Herkles, he keeps a groggery at the corner of the Court."

Mr. Jacob rose, and bidding the dame good night, proceeded to the "Hotel" of a huge negro, who went by the name of Black Herculus or "Herkles," in the more familiar dialect of Moyamensing. Picking his way through the darkness, he presently entered a low and narrow room, filled with stench and smoke, with negroes, men, women, and children huddled together in one corner, and a bar in the other, behind which stood the negro himself dealing out whiskey to a customer. The scene was lighted by three tallow candles stuck in as many porter bottles. The negro was a huge burly fellow, black as the ace of spades, with a mouth like a gash, a nose that looked as if it had been trodden upon, and fists that might have felled an ox. The customer was a white man, rather tall and muscular, dressed in a miserable suit of grey rags, with his hair worn long before his ears, and a greasy cloth cap drawn low over his forehead.

"This 'ere whiskey burns like real ——," grunted the customer, concluding his sentence with a blasphemous expression.

"Dat it does. It am de rale stuff—hot as pepper an' brimstone." After these words "the loafer" in grey rags stretched himself on the floor, and our worthy gentleman approached the negro. A few words sufficed to put the negro in possession of the object of Mr. Jacob Chester's visit. He grinned horribly as the worthy man bent over the counter, and communicated his desire in a confiding whisper.

"Dars my hand on it," he said, "for a small matter o' fifty dollars, Brac Herkles put twenty gals in a cab."

"To-morrow night, remember. The old lady's agreeable and I'll have the cab at the street corner. There's twenty-five on account."

"Y-a-s sah; dats de talk," responded the negro grasping the money.

"Who's that fellow?" whispered Mr. Jacob, touching with his foot the prostrate form of the "loafer," who by this time was snoring lustily.

"Dat,—eh, dat? I raly dono his name—but he's a KILLER."

This seemed perfectly satisfactory to Mr. Jacob who left the groggery and made the best of his way homeward. After his visitor had gone, the negro approached the prostrate loafer, and kicked him with his splay foot.

"Get out o' dis. Dis aint no place for you dam white trash."

CHAPTER VI.

*The mysterious Sign—One man followed by twenty—The Leader
of the Killers—The Den of the Killers.*

THE loafer arose grumbling, and lounged lazily to the door,
which the Black Herkles closed after him, with the objurgation—
"De dam Killers; dar room is better as dar company."

No sooner, however, had the loafer passed from the groggery
into the Court than his lazy walk changed into a brisk stride, his
head rose on his shoulders, and he seemed to have become in a
moment altogether a new man.

He passed from the Court into the street, where a couple of
ruffian-like men, stood beneath the light of the street lamp. As
he approached them, he made a sign with his right hand, and
the two ruffians followed him like dogs obeying the whistle of a
master. Along the dark and deserted street the loafer pursued his
way, until he came to the corner of a well known street leading
from the Delaware to the Schuylkill; a street which, by the bye,
was lighted at every five yards by a groggery or a beer-shop. At the
corner and near the door of every groggery stood groups of men
or half-grown boys—sometimes two and sometimes three or four
in a group. The loafer passed them all, repeating the sign which
he had given to the first two ruffians. And[13] the sign the men and
half-grown boys fell quietly in his wake; by the time he had gone
half a square he was followed by at least twenty persons, who
tracked his footsteps without a word. For a quarter of an hour they
walked on, the silence only broken by the shuffling of their feet.
At length arriving before an unfinished three story brick building

(unfinished on account of the numerous riots which have so long kept the District of Moyamensing in a panic) they silently ranged themselves around the "Loafer" whose sign they had followed.

"All Killers?" he said, anxiously scanning the visage of the ruffians, boys and men, who were only dimly perceptible by the star light.

"All Killers," was the answer.

The "Loafer" jumped through the open cellar door of the unfinished house and in a moment was followed by the twenty. Scrambling through the dark cellar, they ascended in silence into the upper rooms of the unfinished house, and in a few minutes entered an apartment on the third floor. It was brilliantly lighted by a number of candles stuck into porter bottles. The walls were black with tobacco smoke, and ornamented with numerous devices, such as, "Go it Killers! Death to the Bouncers! Killers, No. 1.—Killers No. 2, etcetra. The place was without chair, table, or furniture of any kind. The porter bottles containing the candles were placed at various distances along the uncarpeted floor. Around each candle, seated on the floor, was a group of men and boys, who were drinking whiskey, playing cards and smoking and swearing like so many steam-engines.

This was the "Den of the Killers."

And into this foul den, entered the "Loafer," succeeded by his twenty followers. He was hailed with a shout, "Hurrah for Dick Hellfire, Captain of the Killers!" He answered the shout in as hearty a manner, and then flinging a couple of dollars on the floor added, "Some more rum boys! We may as well make a night of it."

Then looking beneath the front of his cap he silently surveyed "the Killers." They were divided into three classes—beardless apprentice boys who after a hard day's work were turned loose upon the street at night, by their masters or bosses. Young men of nineteen and twenty, who fond of excitement, had assumed the name and joined the gang for the mere fun of the thing, and who would either fight for a man or knock him down, just to keep their hand in; and fellows with countenances that reminded of the brute and devil well intermingled. These last were the smallest in number, but the most ferocious of the three. These, the third class, not more than ten in number, were the very worst specimens of the savage of the large city. Brawny fellows, with faces embruted by hardship, rum and crime; they were "just the boys" to sack a Theatre or burn a Church.

It was to these that Dick Hellfire, the leader of the Killers addressed himself.

"Come lieutenants, let's go into the next room. While the boys have their fun here, we'll cut out some work for to-morrow. To-morrow's 'lection day."

The eleven ruffians rose at his bidding and following[14] him into the next room, the foremost carrying a porter bottle in his hand. There were pieces of carpet huddled up in the corners; there were the beds of the lieutenants, and in this room they slept during the day, after a night of riot and drunkenness. Taking his position in the centre of the room, with the eleven ruffians around him, Dick Hellfire surveyed the hang dog faces in silence, for a few moments, and then began:

"In a week my boys we'll start for Cuba. Cuba, gold and Spanish women, that's our motto! You know that I'm in communication with some of the heads of the expedition; I was told to pick out the most desperate devils I could find in Moyamensin'. I've done so. You've signed your names, and received your first month's pay. In a week you'll go on to New York with me, and then hurrah for Cuba, gold and Spanish women!"

"Hurrah for Cuba, gold and Spanish women!" was the chorus.

Dick Hellfire raised his cap, and displayed a sunburnt face, encircled by sandy whiskers, and with the marks or scar of a frightful wound under the left eye. There was a kind of ferocious beauty about that countenance. It was the face of a man of twenty-three, who had seen and suffered much, and known life on land and sea, in brothel and bar room, and perhaps in the Jail.

"But to-morrow night is election night, and we may as well make a raise before we go." This sentiment was greeted with a chorus of oaths.

"To make a long story short boys, to-morrow night, a rich nabob of Walnut street, who has failed for $200,000; and who carries a great part of his money about him, in fear of his creditors, who would lay hold of houses or lands if he owned either—to-morrow night, this nabod,[15] comes down to that groggery kept by the big nigger—"

"Black Herkles! D—n him," said two voices in a breath.

"He's coming their[16] on some dirty work. Now I move that we set a portion of our gang to raise the devil among the niggers of Mary street, while we watch for the nabob and get hold of him, and bring him to our den."

This sentiment met with a unanimous response. Placing the candle on the floor, Dick squatted beside it, and motioned to the others to follow his example. Presently a circle of "gallows" faces, surrounded the light, with the sunburnt and seamed visage of Dick Hellfire, in the centre.

"He carries some two or three thousand dollars about him," said Dick. "His name is Jacob Chester. Now follow my directions. You Bob will take care and get a police officer or two to help our gang to raise a muss among the niggers. You Jake will head one half of the boys, and first raise an alarm of fire. You Tom will come with me, and hang around Black Herkles groggery to-morrow night after dark. Let's understand one another."

And while he communicated his directions, the shouts and songs of the Killers in the next room, came through the partition, like the yells of so many Texian hunters about to charge a detachment of rancheroes.[17]

CHAPTER VII.

The Great Riot on Election Night, Philadelphia, October 1849.
The Killers.

ELECTION night, October 11, 1849, presented a busy scene in the city and districts of Philadelphia. Bonfires were blazing in every street, crowds of voters collected around every poll, and every groggery and bar-room packed with drunken men. The entire city and county was astir. And a murmur[18] arose from the city, through the stillness of night, like the tramp of an immense army.

There was one district however which presented the details of an excitement altogether peculiar to itself. It was that district which partly comprised in the City proper, and partly in Moyamensing is filled with groggeries, huts, and dens of every grade of pollution, as thick and foul as insects in a tainted cheese. Occupied by many hard working and honest people, the District has for two years been the scene of perpetual outrage. Here, huddled in rooms thick with foul air, and drunk with poison that can be purchased for a-penny a glass, you may see white and black, young and old, men and women, cramped together in crowds that fester with wretchedness, disease and crime. This mass of misery and starvation affords a profitable harvest to a certain class of "hangers on of the law" who skulk about the offices of Aldermen, trade in licenses and do the dirty work which prominent politicians do not care to do for themselves.

Through this district, at an early hour on the night of election, a furniture car, filled with blazing tar barrels, was dragged by a number of men and boys, who yelled like demons, as they whirled their locomotive bonfire through the streets. It was first taken through a narrow street, known as St. Mary street, and principally inhabited by negroes, and distant about one square from the groggery of Black Herkles and the home of the young woman, mentioned in the previous pages. As the car whirled along a shot was fired; a cry at once arose that a white man was shot, and the attention of the mob, was directed to a house at the corner of Sixth and St. Mary, kept by a black fellow who, was rumored to have a white wife. The mob gathered numbers every moment, and a conflict ensued, between the white mob and the negroes, who had fortified themselves within the California house (a four story building) and in the neighbouring tenements and hovels. The inmates after a desperate contest were forced to fly; the bar was destroyed, and the gas set on fire. In a moment the house was in a blaze and the red light flashing against the sky, was answered by the State House bell, which summoned the engine and hose companies to the scene of action. The Hope, the Good Will, the Phœnix, the Vigilant, and other engine companies arrived upon the scene,—amid the clamor of the riot, while pistol shots broke incessantly on the ear, and the flames of burning houses, ascended to the heavens, lighting with a red glare the face of the mob,—and attempted to save the houses, which were yet untouched by the flames. Their efforts were frustrated. The mob took possession of the Hope Hose, and ran it up St. Mary street; as for the other companies, they were greeted at every turn by discharges of fire-arms, loaded with buckshot and slugs. Charles Himmelwright, a fireman of the Good Will, was shot trough[19] the heart, while nobly engaged in the discharge of his duty. He was a young and honest man. He fell dead the moment he received the shot. Many were wounded, and many killed. It was an infernal scene. The faces of the mob reddened by the glare, the houses whirling in flames, the streets slippery with blood, and a roar like the yells of a thousand tigers let loose upon their prey, all combined gave the appearance of a sacked and ravaged town, to the District which spreads around Sixth and St. Mary street. The rioters and spectators on the streets were not the only sufferers. Men and women sheltered within their homes, were shot by the stray missiles of the cowardly combatants.

CHAPTER VIII.

Black Herkles—Ophelia—Mr. Jacob Chester—Chloroform—
The father and son.

WHILE scenes like these were progressing, and while the troops of approaching soldiers was heard, all was quiet as the grave in the vicinity of the "groggery" kept by Black Herkles. The huts of the court were either deserted or closed; and every tenement looked as though it had not been occupied for a month, with two exceptions. There was a light in the groggery of Black Herkles, and in the home of the old woman and her daughter.

Black Herkles was standing at his door, with folded arms the light from within playing over one side of his hideous face, when footsteps were heard from the further extremity of the Court, and a female figure was seen approaching through the glass. It was the poor girl, Ophelia Thompson, "the supernumerary" on her way to the theatre. With her shawl thrown over her shoulders, and her veil drooped over her face, she came along with a hesitating step, pausing every moment as if to listen to the noise of the conflict which was progressing at the distance of not more than two hundred yards.

She came on; the light from the groggery shone over her tall form; she passed, when a hand was laid upon her mouth, and her arms were pinioned to her side, by an arm that encircled her with a grasp of iron. She attempted to scream, but in vain. She struggled, but the iron-arm held her arms firmly against her sides. Tossing back her head in her struggles, she beheld with a horror that no words can paint, the black visage of the negro.

It may be as well to observe that the events of the night had in some measure changed the plan of Mr. Jacob Chester and the negro. Instead of placing the cab at the corner of the Court, they had placed it in a neighbouring street, which communicates with the back door of the groggery, by means of a narrow alley. Therefore Black Herkles bore the struggling girl into his bar-room, and from the bar-room into a room in the second story, where waited Mr. Jacob Chester, anxious to confront his victim, ere he had her conveyed to the cab. He designed to have her kept within this room, until the riot would reach its height, and the additional confusion serve to render his passage to a mansion in "the neck,"[20] (which he had rented for the purpose) near Gray's Ferry, at once convenient and safe. The negro ascended the stairs, applied a bit of rag wet with some pungent liquid to the lips of the girl, and the next moment, tumbled her insensible form into the room, where Mr. Jacob Chester waited. The liquid was chloroform.

This accomplished the negro descended, hurried along the alley and saw that the cab stood there in the street, according to the plan agreed upon. He then returned to his bar-room, which he had entirely cleared of its usual customers, an hour before. Busying himself behind the bar he was surprised by the entrance of the "loafer" in the grey rags, whom he had ejected the night previous. In his African dialect, he bade the fellow quit his premises, but the "loafer" whined piteously for a glass of whiskey, which Black Herkles at last consented to give him.

As he poured out the liquid poison, the "loafer" leaned over the counter, one hand upon a large earthen pitcher supposed to contain water.

"Dars yer whiskey. Take it and trabel," said Herkles, pushing the glass toward his customer. The loafer raised his glass slowly to his lips, and at the same time kept his hand upon the handle of the pitcher, but instead of drinking the poison he dashed it in the negro's eyes, at the same time hurling the pitcher, with all the force of his arm, at his head. Blinded by the liquor, half-stunned by the blow, Black Herkles uttered a frightful howl, and attempted to "get at" his antagonist across the bar. But a second blow, administered with a "slung-shot" which the "loafer" drew from his rags, took the negro in the forehead, and laid him flat upon the floor.

The moment that he fell, the room was filled with "Killers" who surrounded their leader, known as the "loafer," or "Dick Hell-fire," with shouts and cries. They were eleven in number, whom Dick had instructed the night before. Drunken, furious, and brutal, they were about to beat and mangle the prostrate negro, when Dick stopped them with a word.

"Look here, boys." The devil's delight is up at St. Mary street, and we must be busy while the fun lasts. Four of you go to the end of the alley, and take care of the cab; two of you guard the front door, and let the rest remain outside, on the watch, while I go up stairs. When I whistle ALL come. I'll go up and see the old fellow and his gal."

He was implicitly obeyed. Four of the Killers hastened through the back door; two remained in the bar-room, and the rest went out into the Court. Pausing for a moment ere he ascended the dark stairway Dick Hellfire wiped from his hands the blood which he had received in the conflict, near the California House, for he had been in the thickest of the fight. Then casting a glance toward the prostrate form of the negro stretched behind the bar, his forehead covered with blood, Dick crept up the stairs and placed his ear against the door at the head of the flight. All was still within. Dick pushed open the door and entered. By the light of a candle, Mr. Jacob Chester, hat and overcoat thrown aside, was contemplating the form of the insensible girl, who was stretched upon a miserable bed. Her hair fell in disorder about her neck; her eyes were closed and her lips parted; she looked extremely beautiful, but it was a beauty like death. And over her, his bald head shining in the light, stood the aged sinner, his eyes fixed upon his unconscious victim, and his mouth parting in a salacious grin. The noble form of the poor girl was stretched before him—in his power,—in a few hours she would be safe within his mansion near Gray's Ferry. Thus occupied he had not heard the opening of the door, nor was he aware of the presence of Dick, until that personage laid a hand upon his arm, saying mildly,

"How d'ye do father."

The surprise of Mr. Jacob Chester may be imagined. Turning he beheld the stalwart figure, clad in rags, which were stained with blood. The cap drawn over the brow concealed the upper part of the whiskered face. Mr. Jacob could not believe his eyes. He started as though he had received a musket shot.

Dick removed his cap.

"I heard that having become aware of my return from Havana, you put a police officer on my track. Here I am. Now what do you want with me?"

Mr. Jacob Chester grew pale; he could not speak. He gazed at Dick Hellfire, otherwise known as Charles Anderson Chester, with eyes that seemed about to fall from their sockets.

"Come father, it really won't do. You must really give me that belt about your waist, or I'll have to be cross with you. I've been in rough scenes since you kicked me out of the store, and am not disposed to stand on trifles. Strip!"

Mr. Jacob Chester unbuttoned his vest, and took from beneath his shirt a leather belt, which to all appearance, contained a considerable amount in specie.

"It's all I have in the world. Take that and I'm a beggar," he faltered. Charles took the belt, unlocked it, and having ascertained that it contained gold and bank notes, he locked it again and fastened it about his waist. As for the old man he watched his movements with a stupified gaze.

"Now I'll just wake the girl and leave you to your meditations," said Dick *alias* Charles, and approaching the bed, he laid his hand upon the hand of Ophelia Thompson. He started as he encountered the touch of that hand. Again he seized it, and dropped it, as though its contact had filled him with inexpressible terror. When he turned his face towards the old man, it was lived[21] with horror.

"By G—d, old man you're worse than I thought you was!" he cried, and staggered to the door, leaving Mr. Jacob Chester alone with the dead girl. She had been killed by the chloroform.

CHAPTER IX.

The Stab—Black Herkles at bay—The Killers take signal vengeance—The figure on the house top—The double death.

DESCENDING the stairway, he felt the belt which encircled his waist, in order to assure himself that it was safe, and was passing into the bar-room, when he received a violent blow upon the breast.

He never lived to know the cause of that blow. For a large knife had sunk to the hilt in his left breast: he was stabbed to the heart, he uttered one groan and fell a dead man. And over him, triumphant and chuckling stood Black Herkles, the knife dripping in his hand. He wiped the blood from his mangled brow, and stamped upon the dead body, in the extremity of his rage.

The cause of the scene is readily explained. An alarm at the corner of the street and court, had summoned the Killers from the scene, but a moment after Charles ascended the stairs. Neglecting their posts, they had hurried to join in the affray at the street corner. They were only absent a few moments. During their absence the negro had recovered from the effects of the blow, and seizing a knife, waited for Charles, as he heard him descending the stairs.

When the comrades of "Dick" alias "Charles" returned they found the negroes[22] standing in one corner, the bloody knife in his right hand, and his foot planted upon the breast of the dead man.

"Come on you dam Killers," he bawled,—"I've stuck your bully, and I'm ready for de wust of you!"

The surprise of the Killers may be imagined. It was not their intention to fight the infuriated negro. Whispering together, they retreated from the room, half of their number went round to the back of the groggery, while the other half watched the front of the door. That door and the back door together with the windows, they closed, fastened and nailed; sending one of their number to the corner of Sixth and Mary for reinforcements. In less than fifteen minutes the groggery was in a blaze, and by the flames, the faces of a thousand combatants were visible. The riot had swelled like a wave from the corner of Sixth and Mary to the court, at the corner of which was situated the groggery of Black Herkles. And when the firemen attempted to play upon the burning pile, they were beaten back, shot and maimed by the rioters, among the most demoniac of whom, were the comrades of Charles Anderson Chester. A sound came from the burning house; it was the yell of the negro imprisoned in the flames.

"There's a man in that house," roared twenty voices.

"Let him burn," answered the Killers.

The contest was renewed; negroes and whites were fighting in the narrow court, and the flames, mounting to the roof, began to communicate with the adjoining huts. In the midst of the scene, a dark and gigantic figure, appeared on the roof of the groggery, environed by flames, and bearing the form of a woman in his arms. A yell of horror from a thousand voices, was heard at the sight. He stood there for a moment, and then the roof fell beneath him, and his burden fell like lead upon the pavement.

It was the dead body of Ophelia Thompson.

As the crowd gave way, one shuddering pervaded every heart, two figures, hastening from opposite directions approached the corpse.

One was the mother of the dead girl; and the other an old man, whose apparel was burnt to cinder, while his face was horribly marked by the ravages of fire. It was Mr. Jacob Chester, who had escaped through the back window, in time to save his life, though his face was horribly deformed. He and the old woman, formed the centre of the crowd, and looked in silence into the face of the dead girl.

CHAPTER X.

The killed, wounded and arrested.

The riot continued throughout election night. At 6 o'clock, on the ensuing morning the military assembled in force in Independence Square under command of Gen. Patterson and Col. Bohlen. Their approach to the ground, became known, and the Killers, rendered cowardly by the death of their leader, slunk to their den. The following is a list of the killed and wounded:—

KILLED.—Charles Himmelwright, white, shot through the head.

Colored man, unknown, at the hospital.

Ophelia Thompson, white.

WOUNDED.—Mrs. Smith, residing in Sixth street, above South, shot through the head.

Charles Westerhood, residing near the corner 13th and Race streets, thigh fractured by a ball.

Jeremiah M'Shane, shot in the temple, not expected to live.

Jacob Chester, burnt.

Wm. Coleman, shot in the thigh and leg.

Charles Shearer, shot in the leg.

Edward Matthews, shot in two places, the breast and ribs, mortally wounded.

Geo. Williams, shot in the breast.

Augustus Green, shot in the hand and leg.

John Hall, wounded in the neck and arm.

R. Rundel, colored, wounded in the last riot this morning.

Chas. Anderson, colored, shot in the thigh and arm, in the
last conflict.

Here are only a part however of the killed and wounded.

The following persons were arrested: George Hosey, a powerful negro, formerly a dog-catcher. He was arrested after a powerful
resistance: Wm. Shinkle; James Murphy; John McVey; Daniel
Roberts; John Thompson; James Devine; Wm. Jones; John Frit-
zimmons; Joseph Walker; Alex. Cambry; Wm. Simpson; Frank.
C. Riley; James Jones; and Jacob Chester, all white. Also Alex.
Wilson, Jacob Perkins, coloured.

Thus ended one of the most terrible riots which ever disgraced
a civilized city. The facts in the preceding narrative are based
upon the written statements of James Jones, now a convict in the
Penitentiary and the admissions of Mr. Jacob Chester, who did
not long survive the wounds which he received on election night.
James Jones is penitent, and states that he was thrown into the
matter by Charles Chester, the leader of the Killers.

As for Charles, his body was found the second day of the
riot, amid the cinders of the demolished groggery. The belt of
money about his waist, although scorched by the flame was not
altogether destroyed. It fell into the hands of a worthy police officer, who would have kept it to himself had he not been obliged
to buy himself out of the hands of justice.

The funerals of the victims of the riot were attended by a
vast body of citizens, particularly that of the brave Charles Himmelwright, who so nobly fell in the discharge of his duty, shot by
the murderous pistols of the Killers.

That terrible body of outlaws still exists in a broken state, and no one knows how soon their misdeeds may again shock the moral sense of the world. The youth of our land should learn wisdom from the fate of Charles Anderson Chester, the LEADER OF THE KILLERS.

THE END.

APPENDIX 2

Introduction to the Serialized Version of *The Killers*

The Killers, when published serially in the story paper the *Quaker City* (edited by George Lippard), featured the following introduction, which did not appear in the subsequent stand-alone printings of the work. The text is taken from the copy of the *Quaker City* (December 1, 1849, p. 3) held at the Historical Society of Pennsylvania.

"The Killers."
A Narrative

BASED UPON FACTS DEVELOPED
IN A RECENT JUDICIAL INVESTIGATION

Written for the Quaker City.

INTRODUCTION

The Killers! THE KILLERS! THE KILLERS! Who has not heard of the KILLERS? Of their brawls by day, and riots by night? Their robberies in the streets, their fighting in alleys, their house burnings and negro huntings? The very word KILLERS comes back to us, in all the papers of the United States, hurled into the very throats of the Philadelphiana, in the shrilled accents of reproach, and the deepest thunder of horror. Old men and babies—mothers and daughters—girls and boys—throughout the land grow pale at the very mention of the KILLERS. The Killers who get up riots, hunt negroes and burn houses are bad enough. But there are various classes of Killers, and our friends of the Press and Pulpit, in their denunciation of the Rowdy Killers, should not forget that he has brethren, *Respectable* KILLERS. Your Killer is divided into many varieties. There is the Killer who keeps a clothing store, and who kills by paying workwomen 15 cents for making a pair of pantaloons. There is the Killer who puts Labor and the Laborer to a slow death, in the pestilential air of the Factory. There is the Killer, who sits in the Vestry Room of Trinity Church, and who prates smoothly of Religion, while said church holds land to which it has not even the shadow of a title—and while said church owns and lets one mile of houses, dedicated to the damnation of the very soul of Woman. There is the Killer who murders his fellow men in a slow quiet way, by taking advantage of their necessities—by shaving their paper at "two per cent." a month—by selling land from beneath their feet—by renting houses at a price which entails slow starvation upon the renter—by doing a brisk business, in all those forms of body and soul murder, which are comprised under the heads of "Stocks," "Mortgages" and "Ground-Rents." There is the Killer who gets from some pliant or drunken legislature, a Charter to rob so many thousand men and women of their labor and of their bread, by means of copper-plate Lies, commonly called "Bank Notes." This is often the very vilest kind of Killer. He would not do murder in a bold ruffian-like way. No. The sight of blood shocks him. But he does murder in a sneaking, stealthy, snake-like way; and murders men and women who work for their living, by stealing the bread from their table, and the bed from beneath their heads. The Banker Killer, whether called Plainfield or Morris or Susquehanna, may be a very smooth spoken Killer—a "godly" Killer—a Killer observant of all the little proprieties of life—but he is, to tell the truth, the very foulest of his breed. The Killer of Moyamensing, drunk on bad brandy, and filthy with the mud of the kennel—reeking at once with rum and blood—is a decent, honest, and respectable man, compared to his smooth Brother—the Killer who skulks behind the Charter of a Bank. Then there is the Killer on the Bench, who wrenches a bad law to his purpose, and does murder in the name of Coke and Blackstone.[1] A very sneaking Killer, is the Killer on the Bench. Just look at him. There he sits, thin and wiry, with something of the malice of the ape, and something of the wisdom of the owl, printed on his lean visage. Appointed by some Governor, whose tool he had been—to whose political lusts he had been the constant pander—this Killer on the Bench holds every accused person as guilty, even before the formality of a trial—blackguards Juries who are brave enough to be honest—links Poverty in the same breath with Murder—and sends his victims to the Jail or Penitentiary with a sort of glee, that reminds you of a Ghoul chuckling over the corpse which he is about to devour.

—We commend these varieties of the genus KILLER to the notice of the Press throughout the Union, who have been so eloquent upon the Killers of Moyamensing. Come—let us have a paragraph or two about the Respectable Killers. And while you are about it, just say a word in relation to those Killers who sent one generation of Orphans to the street, the jail and the almshouse, in order that Elections might be carried for the benefit of Girard College Conspirators[2]—say a word—one word—about the GIRARD COLLEGE KILLERS.

—And meanwhile, in the Narrative which succeeds this introduction, we shall do our best to render Justice to all kinds of Killers. Whether the Narrative is based on facts or not you will be able to judge after you have read it.

APPENDIX 3

Related Contemporary Documents

The California House Riot was widely covered in the periodical press, and in some cases at great length. Much of the coverage was based on or directly reprinted from Philadelphia newspaper sources such as the *Public Ledger* and the *Inquirer.* Included here are accounts from several periodicals from beyond Philadelphia: the *Baltimore Sun*; the Methodist Episcopal newspaper the *Christian Advocate and Journal*; the Washington, D.C.-based abolitionist weekly the *National Era*; and the African American newspaper the *North Star*, of Rochester, New York.

Also included here is an excerpt from Zachary Taylor's December 24, 1849, message to Congress, part of which is quoted at the end of *The Killers*.

"Dreadful Riot at Philadelphia: Houses Burned, and Several Persons Killed and Wounded"

(*Baltimore Sun*, October 11, 1849)

We gave yesterday morning, by telegraph, a brief account of a terrible riot that was progressing at Philadelphia at the time we went to press. The Philadelphia papers of yesterday morning, due yesterday afternoon, failed, with the exception of the Pennsylvania Inquirer. The letter of our Philadelphia correspondent, due by the boat last night, which we looked for with much interest, has also failed to come to hand. The following notice of the commencement of the riot we extract from the Inquirer:

It is with sincere regret that we record the occurrence of one of the most dreadful and sanguinary riots that has taken place for many years in our city. So far as we have been able to collect the particulars, it appears that a gang of men and boys, amounting it is said to several hundreds, and mostly armed with guns, pistols or knives, hovered about St. Mary's street, which is chiefly inhabited by colored people, and those not of a decent and orderly class, generally speaking. At the same time, there were several knots or crowds of colored men hanging about, and two or three collisions occurred.

This was the state of things shortly after nine o'clock. Before ten, an attack was made upon a tavern at the corner of Sixth and St. Mary's streets, called the California House. This place was kept by a colored man, who was reported to be married, or at any rate, living with a white woman. Whether such were really the case, or merely a rumor, circulated to excite popular indignation, it is not in our power to state. At any rate, the house was soon in flames, the inmates driven out and fired upon, with many other colored persons—men, women and children—who were seen flying from their houses in extreme terror—chased by gangs, who pelted them with brickbats and fired after them with guns and pistols. Several were said to be wounded—and it was stated that more than one was killed. But this report we could not verify. The assailants are described as being composed of the "Killers" and other and similar associations of disturbers of the public peace. Meanwhile the fire made rapid progress—but several Engine and Hose companies were soon upon the ground. And here a truly frightful scene occurred. The firemen who went to the conflagration for the purpose of saving property, were fired upon, not in solitary cases—but actually in a running fire and by volleys of several guns and pistols at once—the rioters being out in very strong force.— They were also assailed with showers of brickbats and their hose cut in every direction. In a word, the first companies that arrived were compelled, as the only mode of avoiding wounds or death, to leave the neighborhood. Still the firing continued. It is impossible to tell the number of killed and wounded, but we saw either five or six carried to druggists' shops or to the Hospital, on chairs or settees. We heard that two were shot while standing on an engine, and one was reported to be killed.

The most moderate statements that were made at 12 o'clock admitted that at least twenty were wounded, and about four killed. Shortly before midnight, a body of police forced their way to the scene of action, fire, and bloodshed, and while standing in Sixth street, below Lombard, we heard at least a dozen shots fired between St. Mary's and South streets, while bricks were showered by the rioters, but as the body of men, which we were told were police, was not repulsed, it was fair to presume that the rioters had given way. Still, the dangerous missiles flew in showers, and at this time, one or two engines and Hose Carriages—the Moyamensing and Hope, as we were informed, were exerting themselves to extinguish the flames. The whole scene was fearful and mournful—a source of real sorrow to every Philadelphian. At the corners of all the streets for many squares, were groups of citizens assembled, anxious for the latest intelligence, and mourning over the insecurity of life and property in that portion of our metropolis.

Barney Himmelwright, a member of the Good Will Hose, reported to have been shot through the heart.

Two other firemen dangerously wounded—one in the head and one in the side. A third wounded in leg.

The military were called out at midnight, and several companies made their appearance on the ground at one o'clock this morning. As late as two o'clock this morning, there was still an immense crowd of people. The military remained on the ground.

It will be seen by a dispatch in another place, that the riots were resumed yesterday morning, and that the military were again called out in great force, and took possession of the ground.

"General Intelligence: Riots at Philadelphia — Loss of Life"
(*Christian Advocate and Journal*, October 18, 1849)

The city of Philadelphia, the scene of so many riots, was on Tuesday night and Wednesday morning of last week the scene of a riotous demonstration, which resulted in the death of three persons, the severely wounding of several, and the burning of four houses. On Tuesday night, at about nine o'clock, the "Killers" made a demonstration against a tavern, known as the California House, at the corner of Sixth and St. Mary's-streets, kept by a black man and a white woman. Apprehending the object of the rioters, the coloured people, residing principally in that locality, armed themselves, and endeavoured to defend the property. A fearful scene of disorder and carnage ensued, and lasted until past midnight. Fire-arms were freely used, and two persons were shot dead upon the ground; a third died on the following day, and a fourth, it is feared, cannot survive. Some twelve or thirteen others were severely injured by pistol or musket balls, during the fighting and firing at the two riots.

The military were called out, but it was some three hours before they could be mustered. As soon as they appeared the crowd dispersed. With great want of forethought the military were sent to their homes. At six o'clock the next morning the rioters again mustered, armed with pistols and guns, which wrought sad havoc, and it was again some hours before the military could be assembled. When they reached the scene the rioters immediately dispersed, but detachments of the military prudently kept possession of the streets to a late hour, and effectually prevented any further disturbances.

When the California House was set on fire, several fire companies turned out; but the rioters opened a fire of pistols and muskets upon them, and compelled them to desist. Subsequently, by the aid of the police, who also were fired upon, the Hope Engine and another succeeded in getting a position whence they could play upon the fire. Four houses, however, were burned down before the flames could be arrested. During Wednesday, the leader—a coloured man, named George Hosey—was arrested and committed on a charge of arson, riot, and murder. Several others were arrested on a charge of riot and committed in default of bail.

Appendix 3

"A Bloody Riot in Philadelphia"

(*National Era*, October 18, 1849)

On the evening of Tuesday, 9th instant, while the police were generally engaged at the State House, a gang of rowdies, styled the "*Killers*," furiously assailed the California House at the corner of St. Mary's and Sixth streets, Philadelphia—a house kept by a mulatto who has a white wife. His friends being on the alert, a desperate fight ensued, but at last "the Killers" broke into the house, destroyed everything before them, and set fire to the building, which was soon wrapped in flames. The inmates fled in all directions, being assaulted with stones and firearms. The struggle was continued out of doors; several adjoining houses caught fire; some policemen, who attempted to restore order, were driven off the ground; the fire companies that had rushed to the scene to put out the fire, were fallen upon by the mob, many of the members were shot down, the hose was cut, and the engines were carried off. Two men were killed on the spot—many others were severely wounded.

At last, the military were summoned; but finding when they arrived on the ground, that the rioters had dispersed, they retired, and, so far as we can learn from the published accounts, the place was left without a guard against a renewal of the riot. As might have been expected, the rioters, who had secreted themselves on the gathering of the military, resumed operations so soon as they could do so with impunity, and at six o'clock next morning the State House bell announced that the presence of the soldiers was again required; but it seems that they did not reach the ground till about nine o'clock, when the rioters again disappeared. In the interval, the colored men, according to the statement of the *North American*, had stubbornly resisted the assaults upon them, and succeeded in arresting several of their assailants, whom they handed over to the police.

The whole transaction is disgraceful to Philadelphia. Property is destroyed, men are murdered, houses are fired, the peace of the whole city is threatened by a gang of ruffians, who, had there been an efficient organization of the police, with vigilant, energetic, faithful officers, might have been seized in the first attempt at violence, and prevented from doing any mischief. For want of this, arson and wholesale murder are committed, and the law is trampled under foot, till it becomes necessary to bring in the military power to restore peace. There is not a city in the Union more shamefully mob-ridden than Philadelphia.

F.D., "Philadelphia"
(*North Star*, October 19, 1849)

The papers give an account of another ferocious mob in this mobocratic city. Its violence was directed against the colored people in the neighborhood of Sixth and St. Thomas' street—a large number of whom are represented as having been wounded, and ten or twelve as having been killed. As usual, the excuse for this bloody outbreak is represented to be the fact that white and colored persons were living in the same families together, and associating on equal terms. One of the papers states that this is a mere pretext. But whether it be true or false it conveys an instructive lesson on the bitterness and baseness of the hatred with which colored people are regarded in Philadelphia. When, in any community, a violation of a mere custom, or a disregard of a particular taste, is esteemed an available excuse for setting aside all law, and for resorting to violence and bloodshed, it shows such custom and taste to be profoundly wedded to the affections of the people; and proves them to be most difficult of eradication.

Slavery and prejudice are, evidently, above law and order in Philadelphia—and we are not surprised that "*the society of killers*" should adduce this reason for every outbreak of which they may be guilty. When the Mayor of Philadelphia informed "the *Hutchinson family*" that "he could not protect them from the violence of a mob if they permitted colored persons to attend their concerts," he gave up the government, the peace, and the property of that disgraced city into the hands of a band of atrocious mobocrats.[1] They took authority from the hands of the Mayor, he virtually telling them that they were to have full liberty to endanger the lives, and to destroy the property of any and all persons who should be found acting in disregard of public taste and prejudice, by associating, in any way, with colored persons—and thus, also, he marked out the people of color for destruction whenever the brutal propensities of base white men should prompt them to the work of murderous outrage.

The authority has gone from the government of Philadelphia; and the struggle will be long and fearful, before it will be regained. Since the burning of Pennsylvania Hall,[2] Philadelphia has been from time to time, the scene of a series of most foul and cruel mobs, waged against the people of color—and it is now justly regarded as one of the most disorderly and insecure cities in the Union. No man is safe—his life—his property—and all that he holds dear, are in the hands of a mob, which may come upon him at any moment—at midnight or mid-day, and deprive him of his all.

Shame upon the guilty city! Shame upon its law-makers, and law administrators!—Philadelphia will never be redeemed from the curse of mobs, until it copies the example set by the government of New York in the late Riots in Astor Place.[3]   —F. D.

"From the Philadelphia Ledger: The Riots – Deplorable Results – The Killed and Wounded"

(*North Star*, October 26, 1849)

We resume the details of the riot from the point at which our account of yesterday broke off.

The rioters ascertaining that the military forces had retired, recommenced their lawless acts, and by daylight, the disturbance was raging furiously. —Some of the rioters jumped the fence above the California House, and set fire to the frame building in the rear of the open space, between it and the dwelling above. The colored population residing in the vicinity commenced moving, when even the females were pelted with stones by the rioters while carrying off articles of furniture. The flames spreading the meanwhile, bro't firemen again to the spot. They sallied down the street, and the rioters retreating before them, the Phoenix was put in service. In a short time, however, the rioters returned, and let fly a volley of bricks, with discharges of fire arms, and the members of the Phoenix were forced to fly from their carriage. The firemen, however, were reinforced by citizens, and returning again to the fire, the Good-Will and Phoenix were put into service, and prevented the further spread of the fire, which at this time had communicated to a row of court houses, running west from Sixth street, the roofs of which were all damaged.

The Robert Morris Hose Company had laid their hose for the purpose of assisting in extinguishing the fire, when the members were beaten off the carriage, and it was taken possession of by the rioters, who ran off the hose, (which was cut by them) and then carried off the apparatus into Moyamensing. It was afterwards restored to the company by John Kneass and some other watchmen of that district. The hose of the Diligent Fire Company was hacked with knives so as to be useless. The State House bell again gave the signal for the assembling of the military. At this time Sixth street from Walnut to Lombard street, and from Lombard to South, the battle of bricks and buckshot was going on with occasional intermissions. By half-past 8 o'clock the tumult had ceased, the rioters having nearly all dispersed, and those remaining could not be distinguished from the spectators with whom they were mingled. Several persons were wounded in the affray, of whom the following were admitted into the Hospital:

James Beasley, a member of the Perseverance Hose Company, received a ball in his breast. He was conveyed to the Hospital, where he remains in a critical condition. He lived in the vicinity of Broad and Arch streets.

Lawrence McShane, while looking out of the window of a house in which his sister lived, was struck in the temple with a chance shot, and received a severe wound which will probably prove fatal.

A young medical student received a ball in his thigh while looking on the affray.

The following colored men were also taken to the Hospital: R. Randall, badly hurt, shot in the back of his head; Chas. Anderson, stabbed in the thigh; and George Tillotson, stabbed in the breast.

A colored boy, in the employ of Sheriff Lelar, had three shots extracted from his leg, which were received while passing Sixth and Lombard streets.

A young man, the son of Capt. Walker, the keeper of a tavern in Seventh below South, was wounded during Tuesday night. A marble fired from a musket struck a rib, and glancing, inflicted a severe flesh wound. The marble was extracted by Mr. Rizer.

The following is the verdict of the coroner's inquest upon the body of Charles Himmelwright: "Charles Himmelwright came to his death by a wound in his breast inflicted by a musket ball, which perforated the heart at the junction of the main artery—the weapon being in the hands of some persons unknown to the jury, on the night of the 9th of October, while the deceased was in the discharge of his duties as a fireman, during the riot at Sixth and St. Mary streets."

The coroner also held an inquest upon the body of John Griffith, the colored boy, mentioned yesterday, as having died at the Hospital from a wound in the head, inflicted by a musket ball.—

The following is the verdict of the jury: "That John Griffith came to his death from a wound in his head by a ball from a musket, fired in the hands of some person unknown to the jury, on the night of the 9th of Oct., during the riots at the corner of Sixth and St. Mary streets."

Cornelius Speed, one of the election judges in Sixth Ward, Southwark, was struck on the forehead with a spent ball. The injury was not serious.

The colored church in Lombard st. below 6th, and the old church edifice at Fifth and Gaskill streets, have been converted into barracks for the use of the military.

With the exception of several discharges of fire-arms in Moyamensing, apparently intended for signals by the rioters, no disturbance occurred last evening. In visiting the scene of the late disturbance, we found the streets in the vicinity completely deserted, the rain having had the effect of driving the rioters as well as the spectators to their homes.

McShane died at the hospital last evening about dark. This makes the third fatal case. He had arrived in this country but a few weeks since, and was making preparations to return, intending to start the last of this week.

Arrest for rioting. — During Tuesday night and yesterday, thirty men and boys, black and white, were arrested and committed to the city lock up, on the charge of having been engaged in the riots. Five of them were subsequently discharged. Those in custody will have a hearing today or to-morrow.

The outbreak was one of those sudden explosions of brutal passions, which could not have been foreseen, and owing to the employment of the police force on duties incident to the election, could not be guarded against. —Still the public authorities of the country are justly censurable for allowing a lawless gang of ruffians to gain, by impunity for former frequent outrages, the audacity that showed itself in the resistance they made to the laws on Tuesday night. The rioters have been guilty of the highest crimes known to the laws—arson and murder—and we suggest whether it is not the duty of the Governor to immediately offer a reward for the arrest and conviction of every individual known to have had a hand in the outrage.

Zachary Taylor, Excerpt from *Message from the President of the United States to the Two Houses of Congress, at the Commencement of the First Session of the Thirty-First Congress*

(Washington, D.C.: Printed for the House of Representatives, 1849), pp. 3–16.

Fellow-citizens of the Senate and House of Representatives:

Sixty years have elapsed since the establishment of this government, and the Congress of the United States again assembles to legislate for an empire of freemen. The predictions of evil prophets, who formerly pretended to foretell the downfall of our institutions, are now remembered only to be derided, and the United States of America at this moment present to the world the most stable and permanent government on earth.

Such is the result of the labors of those who have gone before us. Upon Congress will eminently depend the future maintenance of our system of free government, and the transmission of it unimpaired to posterity.

We are at peace with all the other nations of the world, and seek to maintain our cherished relations of amity with them. During the past year we have been blessed, by a kind Providence, with an abundance of the fruits of the earth; and, although the destroying angel, for a time, visited extensive portions of our territory with the ravages of a dreadful pestilence, yet the Almighty has at length deigned to stay his hand, and to restore the inestimable blessing of general health to a people who have acknowledged his power, deprecated his wrath, and implored his merciful protection.

While enjoying the benefits of amicable intercourse with foreign nations, we have not been insensible to the distractions and wars which have prevailed in other quarters of the world. It is a proper theme of thanksgiving to Him who rules the destinies of nations, that we have been able to maintain, amidst all these contests, an independent and neutral position towards all belligerent Powers. . . .

Having been apprized that a considerable number of adventurers were engaged in fitting out a military expedition, within the United States, against a foreign country, and believing, from the best information I could obtain, that it was destined to invade the island of Cuba, I deemed it due to the friendly relations existing between the United States and Spain—to the treaty between the two nations—to the laws of the United States, and, above all, to the American honor—to exert the lawful authority of this government in suppressing the expedition and preventing the invasion. To this end, I issued a proclamation, enjoining it upon the officers of the United States, civil and military, to use all lawful means within their power. A copy of that proclamation is herewith submitted. The expedition has been suppressed. So long as the act of Congress of the 20th of April, 1818,[4] which owes its existence to the law of nations and to the policy of Washington himself, shall remain on our statute book, I hold it to be the duty of the Executive faithfully to obey its injunctions. . . .

The extension of the coast of the United States on the Pacific, and the unexampled rapidity with which the inhabitants of California especially are increasing in numbers, have imparted new consequence to our relations with the other countries whose territories border upon that ocean. It is probable that the intercourse between those countries and our possessions in that quarter, particularly with the republic of Chili, will become extensive and mutually advantageous in proportion as California and Oregon shall increase in population and wealth.[5] It is desirable, therefore, that this government should do everything in its power to foster and strengthen its relations with those States, and that the spirit of amity between us should be mutual and cordial.

I recommend the observance of the same course towards all other American States. The United States stand as the great American power, to which, as their natural ally and friend, they will always be disposed first to look for mediation and assistance, in the event of any collision between them and any European nation. As such, we may often kindly mediate in their behalf, without entangling ourselves in foreign wars or unnecessary controversies. Whenever the faith of our treaties with any of them shall require our interference, we must necessarily interpose.

A convention has been negotiated with Brazil, providing for the satisfaction of American claims on that government, and it will be submitted to the Senate. Since the last session of Congress, we have received an envoy extraordinary and minister plenipotentiary from that empire, and our relations with it are founded upon the most amicable understanding.

Your attention is earnestly invited to an amendment of our existing laws relating to the African slave-trade, with a view to the effectual suppression of that barbarous traffic. It is not to be denied that this trade is still, in part, carried on by means of vessels built in the United States, and owned or navigated by some of our citizens. The correspondence between the Department of State and the minister and consul of the United States at Rio de Janeiro, which has from time to time been laid before Congress, represents that it is a customary device to evade the penalties of our laws by means of sea-letters. Vessels sold in Brazil, when provided with such papers by the consul, instead of returning to the United States for a new register, proceed at once to the coast of Africa, for the purpose of obtaining cargoes of slaves. Much additional information, of the same character, has recently been transmitted to the Department of State. It has not been considered the policy of our laws to subject an American citizen, who, in a foreign country, purchases a vessel built in the United States, to the inconvenience of sending her home for a new register, before permitting her to proceed on a voyage. Any alteration of the laws which might have a tendency to impede the free transfer of property in vessels between our citizens, or the free navigation of those vessels between different parts of the world, when employed in lawful commerce, should be well and cautiously considered; but I trust that your wisdom will devise a method by which our general policy, in this respect, may be preserved, and at the same time the abuse of our flag, by means of sea-letters, in the manner indicated, may be prevented. . . .

. . . Our government can only be preserved in its purity by the suppression and entire elimination of every claim or tendency of one co-ordinate branch to encroachment upon another. With the strict observance of this rule and the other injunctions of the constitution; with a sedulous inculcation of that respect and love for the Union of the States which our fathers cherished and enjoined upon their children; and with the aid of that overruling Providence which has so long and so kindly guarded our liberties and institutions, we may reasonably expect to transmit them, with their innumerable blessings, to the remotest posterity.

But attachment to the Union of the States should be habitually fostered in every American heart. For more than half a century, during which kingdoms and empires have fallen, this Union has stood unshaken. The patriots who formed it have long since descended to the grave; yet still it remains, the proudest monument to their memory, and the object of affection and admiration with every one worthy to bear the American name. In my judgment, its dissolution would be the greatest of calamities; and to avert that should be the study of every American. Upon its preservation must depend our own happiness and that of countless generations to come. Whatever dangers may threaten it, I shall stand by it and maintain it in its integrity to the full extent of the obligations imposed and the power conferred upon me by the constitution.

Z. TAYLOR.

WASHINGTON, December 4, 1849.[6]

NOTES

INTRODUCTION

1   [John Bell Bouton], *The Life and Choice Writings of George Lippard, with a Portrait and Fac-simile of a Portion of a Letter Written in the Early Part of His Illness* (New York: H. H. Randall, 1855), 28.

2   David S. Reynolds, *George Lippard* (Boston: Twayne, 1982), 102. Subsequent citations to Reynolds, *George Lippard* (1982) refer to this edition.

3   George Lippard, *New York: Its Upper Ten and Lower Million* (Cincinnati: H. M. Rulison, 1853), xi.

4   David S. Reynolds, ed., *George Lippard, Prophet of Protest: Writings of an American Radical, 1822–1854* (New York: Peter Lang, 1986), 4–5; see also introduction to George Lippard, *The Quaker City; or, The Monks of Monk Hall: A Romance of Philadelphia Life, Mystery, and Crime*, ed. David S. Reynolds (Amherst: University of Massachusetts Press, 1995). Subsequent parenthetical citations to *The Quaker City* refer to this edition.

5   David S. Reynolds, "Radical Sensationalism: George Lippard in His Transatlantic Contexts," in *Transatlantic Sensations*, ed. Jennifer Phegley, John Cyril Barton, and Kristin N. Huston (Burlington, Vt.: Ashgate, 2012), 77–96, 78.

6   Reynolds, *George Lippard* (1982), 53.

7   David S. Reynolds, *Beneath the American Renaissance: The Subversive Imagination in the Age of Emerson and Melville* (New York: Oxford University Press, 1988), 198–99. David M. Stewart, *Reading and Disorder in Antebellum America* (Columbus: Ohio State University Press, 2011), argues that works like Lippard's should be regarded as not merely about but in fact a part of leisure and labor in the city, woven into a complex reconfiguration of urban life and reading. "The productive rationalization of antebellum working life caused stress," Stewart posits, "which reading helped relieve by producing city crime as a source of negative or nonproductive pleasure" (48).

8   Reynolds, *George Lippard* (1982), 107. Brown was the dedicatee of the first bound version of *The Quaker City*; when originally issued in parts, the first dedicatee was Augustine J. H. Duganne (1823–84), an American poet, novelist, and playwright. Duganne's novel *The Two Clerks; or, The Orphan's Gratitude: Being the Adventures of Henry Fowler and Richard Martin* (Boston: Brainard, 1843) is considered by some to be the earliest American example of the city-mysteries genre.

9   Reynolds, *George Lippard* (1982), 102.

10   For an extended consideration of the literary influence of Lippard on American Renaissance writers and moral best sellers alike, see Reynolds, *Beneath the American Renaissance*. For Reynolds, "the simultaneous appearance between 1850 and 1855 of great Conventional best-sellers . . . and of the central literary texts of the American

Renaissance can be explained . . . as a direct response to the vulgarization of radical-democrat ideals" such as those enacted in Lippard's writings. "Conventional novels tried to fabricate a world of piety and domesticity that rhetorically repaired the shattered, amoral world summoned up by the radical democrats; major works such as *The Scarlet Letter* and *Moby-Dick* . . . boldly absorbed the paradoxes of the radical-democrat imagination but invested them with a new intensity and artistry that rescued them from their increasing crassness and formlessness" (*Beneath the American Renaissance*, 194). For a claim that Whitman's poetry, and in particular the early "Resurgemus" treating the revolutions of 1848, was influenced by Lippard, see Reynolds, *Walt Whitman's America: A Cultural Biography* (New York: Vintage, 1995), esp. 130–32.

11   Roger Butterfield, "George Lippard and His Secret Brotherhood," *Pennsylvania Magazine of History and Biography* 79.3 (July 1955): 285–309, 297–98; and Shelley Streeby, "Haunted Houses: George Lippard, Nathaniel Hawthorne, and Middle-Class America," *Criticism* (Summer 1996): 443–72, 448.

12   Reynolds, *George Lippard* (1982), 18.

13   For a broad picture of American literary reactions to the revolutions of 1848, see Larry J. Reynolds, *European Revolutions and the American Literary Renaissance* (New Haven, Conn.: Yale University Press, 1988).

14   Reynolds, *George Lippard: Prophet of Protest*, 37.

15   *Quaker City* (newspaper), September 29, 1849.

16   Samuel Otter, *Philadelphia Stories: America's Literature of Race and Freedom* (New York: Oxford University Press, 2010), 3.

17   Shelley Streeby, "Opening Up the Story Paper: George Lippard and the Construction of Class," *boundary 2* 24.1 (Spring 1997): 177–203, 182, 192.

18   John Cyril Barton and Jennifer Phegley, "Introduction: 'An Age of Sensation . . . Across the Atlantic,'" in Phegley, Barton, and Huston, *Transatlantic Sensations*, 1–22, 6.

19   Ibid., 16.

20   Paul Christian Jones, *Against the Gallows: Antebellum American Writers and the Movement to Abolish Capital Punishment* (Iowa City: University of Iowa Press, 2011), 75–76.

21   Norman Johnston, "The World's Most Influential Prison: Success or Failure?" *Prison Journal* 84.4 Suppl. (December 2004): 20–40, 20.

22   Ibid., 25.

23   David S. Reynolds, *Waking Giant: America in the Age of Jackson* (New York: HarperCollins, 2008), 211.

24   Caleb Smith, *The Prison and the American Imagination* (New Haven, Conn.: Yale University Press, 2009), 63.

25   Elizabeth Erbeznik, "Workers and Wives as Legible Types in Eugène Sue's *Les Mystères de Paris*," *Nineteenth-Century French Studies* 41 (Fall–Winter 2012–13): 66–79, 71.

26   For a detailed look at the publication history of *The Killers*, and a refutation of Roger Butterfield's claim that Lippard may not have been the author of *Charles Anderson Chester*, see David Faflik, "Authorship, Ownership, and the Case for *Charles Anderson Chester*," *Book History* 11 (2008): 149–67. See also Butterfield, "A Check List

of the Separately Published Works of George Lippard," *Pennsylvania Magazine of History and Biography* 79.3 (1955): 308; and Jacob Blanck, comp., "George Lippard," in *Bibliography of American Literature*, ed. Jacob Blanck, Virginia L. Smyers, and Michael Winship (New Haven, Conn.: Yale University Press, 1969), 5:405–18. See the "Note on the Text" for citation information for the sources consulted for this edition.

27   One-page advertisement for *Life and Adventures of Charles Anderson Chester*, n.d. [ca. 1850], Library Company of Philadelphia, sm # Am 1850 Just 16974.Q (Doret).

28   See Michael Winship, "In Search of Monk-Hall: A Publishing History of George Lippard's *Quaker City*," conference presentation, Society for the History of Authorship, Readership, and Publishing, Philadelphia, July 21, 2013.

29   Those of which we are aware are held at the University of Virginia, the Library of Congress, the American Antiquarian Society, the Library Company of Philadelphia, Yale University, the Ohio State University, the New York Public Library, and the Historical Society of Pennsylvania.

30   Reynolds, *Beneath the American Renaissance*, 208.

31   Daniel R. Biddle and Murray Dubin, *Tasting Freedom: Octavius Catto and the Battle for Equality in Civil War America* (Philadelphia: Temple University Press, 2010), 112–13.

32   John C. McWilliams, "'Men of Colour': Race, Riots, and Black Firefighters' Struggle for Equality from the AFA to the Valiants," *Journal of Social History* (Fall 2007): 105–25, 110.

33   Otter, *Philadelphia Stories*, 204.

34   Harry C. Silcox, *Philadelphia Politics from the Bottom Up: The Life of Irishman William McMullen, 1824–1901* (Philadelphia: Balch Institute Press, 1989), 27; and Biddle and Dubin, *Tasting Freedom*, 116.

35   Otter, *Philadelphia Stories*, 137.

36   F.D., "Philadelphia," *North Star*, October 19, 1849.

37   "A Bloody Riot in Philadelphia," *National Era*, October 18, 1849.

38   "The Philadelphia Riots Again," *North Star*, October 26, 1849.

39   Ibid.

40   "Riots at Philadelphia—Loss of Life," *Christian Advocate and Journal*, October 18, 1849.

41   See Appendix 3 for examples of published lists of casualties from the California House Riot.

42   James Williams, *Fugitive Slave in the Gold Rush: Life and Adventures of James Williams* (Lincoln: University of Nebraska Press, 2002), 7, 8.

43   Timothy Helwig, "Denying the Wages of Whiteness: The Racial Politics of George Lippard's Working-Class Protest," *American Studies* 47.3/4 (Fall–Winter 2006): 87–111, 87; and Harry Hazel [Justin Jones], "Author's Preface" to *Big Dick, the King of the Negroes; or, Virtue and Vice Contrasted* (Boston: Star Spangled Banner Office, 1846). See also Eric Lott, *Love and Theft: Blackface Minstrelsy and the American Working Class* (New York: Oxford University Press, 1993), for the claim that in Lippard's works, "when structured along acceptable class lines—when, that is, there was an implicit twinning of blacks and working-class whites—black characters . . . could be portrayed in liberatory ways" (80).

44 Otter, *Philadelphia Stories*, 193.

45 "Riot in Norristown—Outrage Upon the People of Color," *North Star*, November 16, 1849.

46 F.D., "Philadelphia"; and Otter, *Philadelphia Stories*, 133.

47 Silcox, *Philadelphia Politics*, 27, 30–31. For a longer history of racial demographics and Philadelphia's topography, see Gary Nash, *Forging Freedom: The Formation of Philadelphia's Black Community, 1720–1840* (Cambridge, Mass.: Harvard University Press, 1991).

48 Otter, *Philadelphia Stories*, 137, 9–10.

49 Ibid., 168–69.

50 Mifflin Wistar Gibbs, *Shadow and Light: An Autobiography* (Lincoln: University of Nebraska Press, 1995), 19.

51 Ibid., 23.

52 Streeby, "Haunted Houses," 446.

53 *Quaker City*, March 3, 1849, cited in Streeby, "Opening Up the Story Paper," 192.

54 Helwig, "Denying the Wages of Whiteness," 94. See also Timothy Helwig, "Race, Nativism, and the Making of Class in Antebellum City-Mysteries" (Ph.D. diss., University of Maryland, 2006).

55 Joseph Jackson, "George Lippard: Misunderstood Man of Letters," *Pennsylvania Magazine of History and Biography* 59.4 (October 1935): 376–91, 383.

56 Streeby, "Opening Up the Story Paper," 178.

57 Helwig, "Denying the Wages of Whiteness," 98–99.

58 Sari Altschuler and Aaron M. Tobiason, "Introduction to Playbill for George Lippard's *The Quaker City*," *PMLA* (March 2014). The play, ultimately titled *The Monks of Monk Hall*, eventually saw production in New York City in January 1845.

59 Biddle and Dubin, *Tasting Freedom*, 133.

60 Ibid.; and Alfred Lanore (holds copyright), *The Almighty Dollar; or, The Brilliant Exploits of a Killer* (Philadelphia: Zieber, 1847), 15, 13. Subsequent parenthetical citations to *The Almighty Dollar* refer to this edition.

61 In reality, the California House Riot began on October 9.

62 Helwig, "Denying the Wages of Whiteness," 99.

63 H. C. Watson, "Preface" to *Jerry Pratt's Progress; or, Adventures in the Hose House, Founded on Facts* (Philadelphia: Thomas M. Scroggy, 1855), 5.

64 Charles Godfrey Leland, *Memoirs* (New York: D. Appleton, 1893), 216–17.

65 Biddle and Dubin, *Tasting Freedom*, 125, 127, 130; and Harry C. Silcox, *Letters from an Irish Ward Leader: William McMullen to Samuel J. Randall 1864–1890* (n.p., 1985).

66 Silcox, *Philadelphia Politics*, 49. According to Biddle and Dubin, in 1842, the Moyamensing district alone boasted 450 liquor dealers, most of them Irish (*Tasting Freedom*, 121).

67 Biddle and Dubin, *Tasting Freedom*, 190; and Silcox, *Philadelphia Politics*, 49.

68 Silcox, *Philadelphia Politics*, 41.

69 Kirsten Silva Gruesz, *Ambassadors of Culture: The Transamerican Origins*

of Latino Writing (Princeton, N.J.: Princeton University Press, 2002), 87. See also Reginald Horsman, *Race and Manifest Destiny: The Origins of American Racial Anglo-Saxonism* (Cambridge, Mass.: Harvard University Press, 1981).

70   Silcox, *Philadelphia Politics*, 42.

71   Shelley Streeby, "American Sensations: Empire, Amnesia, and the US-Mexican War," *American Literary History* 13.1 (Spring 2001): 1–40, 8.

72   Gruesz, *Ambassadors of Culture*, 117.

73   Ibid., 143.

74   "The Scheme Unfolding—The Future," *National Era*, August 12, 1847.

75   "Negotiation Concerning the Annexation of Cuba—Extraordinary Disclosures," *National Era*, April 5, 1849.

76   Gruesz, *Ambassadors of Culture*, 144.

77   "New York Correspondence," *National Era*, September 6, 1849.

78   "Matters Relating to Cuba," *National Era*, September 20, 1849.

79   Rodrigo Lazo, "'La Famosa Filadelfia': The Hemispheric American City and Constitutional Debates," in *Hemispheric American Studies*, ed. Caroline Levander and Robert S. Levine (New Brunswick, N.J.: Rutgers University Press, 2008), 57–74, 57–58.

80   "Cuba," *National Era*, February 15, 1849.

81   "Negotiation Concerning the Annexation of Cuba—Extraordinary Disclosures," *National Era*, April 5, 1849.

82   Martin R. Delany, "Annexation of Cuba," *North Star*, April 27, 1849.

83   Ibid.

84   Streeby, "American Sensations," 1–2.

85   Otter, *Philadelphia Stories*, 190.

86   Streeby, "American Sensations," 9.

87   [Bouton], *Life and Choice Writings*, 44.

88   Otter, *Philadelphia Stories*, 190.

89   [Bouton], *Life and Choice Writings*, 126.

THE KILLERS

1   New Haven, Connecticut, was known as the "Elm City" thanks to an early civic tree-planting initiative.

2   Cuban cigars; named for Havana.

3   Saratoga Springs, New York, was a popular resort in the early nineteenth century.

4   John Jacob Astor (1763–1848) was a wealthy fur trader and real-estate magnate, and the first U.S.-based multimillionaire.

5   Lovejoy's Hotel was just off Broadway on Park Row, in a popular entertainment district that included among other attractions Barnum's American Museum.

6   The Chatham Street Theatre was on Chatham between James and Roosevelt Streets in New York City, not far from the abovementioned Lovejoy's Hotel.

7   Cape May was and remains a popular coastal New Jersey resort town, visited by many well-off Philadelphians looking to escape the heat of the city during the summer.

8   Cognac.

9   Meaning, of the fashionable aristocratic elite, short for *bon ton*.

10   A sight draft, like a check, is a note payable when presented to a bank; it can be dated for payment, as referenced later in the narrative ("drafts at one, two and three days sight").

11   After Oliver Cromwell (1599–1658), controversial Puritan military leader of the Parliamentary forces in the English Civil War of the seventeenth century, and Lord Protector of Britain from 1653 to 1658.

12   Probably intended to be "carcass."

13   Laudanum is a liquid medical preparation of opium, used in the nineteenth century to treat a range of illnesses. Its narcotic effects and addictiveness were notorious.

14   Eastern State Penitentiary (also known early on as "Cherry Hill") opened on October 23, 1829, though in its originally planned dimensions was not actually completed until 1836. Its controversial system of solitary confinement, theorized to induce repentance and internal reformation, became known as the "Pennsylvania System" or the "separate system"; prisons modeled on Eastern State were built across the globe, and it was a significant tourist attraction.

15   Probably intended to be "clerk."

16   Currencies were, as this question suggests, local to states and occasionally cities in the United States until after the Civil War. Later, when Cromwell is told that "the very bank notes which you have about you will betray you," he is being reminded that his act of forgery can be traced because of the specific origins of the specie he has been given in exchange for the sight drafts intended for his father.

17   A tidal strait connecting Upper New York Bay and Lower New York Bay, the main passage by water from New York City to the Atlantic Ocean.

18   In the nineteenth-century United States, "Potter's Field" denominated a common burial ground for unknown or deprecated people. See, in the Bible, Jeremiah 19:11 and Matthew 27:7–10.

19   Probably intended to be "Eastern."

20   An early brand of matches ignited by friction.

21   Probably intended to be "beaded."

22   An ornate chest containing the stone tablets on which the Ten Commandments were written. See in the Bible, for a start, Exodus 25:10–22.

23   Hicks's banks, discussed above, were known as "wildcat banks," which were state chartered and often located in rural areas in which it was difficult for account holders to redeem notes rapidly, allowing for quick liquidation of the bank when rates favored bank owners. Protection for individual bank account holdings was not instituted until the establishment of the Federal Deposit Insurance Corporation in 1933.

24   Abbreviation for "manuscripts."

25   A heavy overcoat; presumably in this case with a large collar.

26   Fanny Kemble (1809–93) was a famous British actress and author. At the time *The Killers* was published, Kemble had recently made a major tour of the United States and had also divorced her husband, Pierce Butler (1810–67).

27   Elections were held October 9, 1849, in Philadelphia; all of these elections were for local offices.

28   "Bulgine," or "bullgine," was a popular term for a locomotive or steam engine.

29   Repeated in original.

30   Probably intended to be "visitor."

31   Repeated in original.

32   Charles Langfeldt was executed on October 20, 1848, for the murder of Catherine Rademacher. Langfeldt had recently been released from Eastern State Penitentiary, and maintained that he was innocent of the murder.

33   Probably "magic lanterns," which produced projected images from painted glass slides.

34   Repeated in original.

35   A short loop of rope with a heavy weight on one end, used in seafaring contexts to toss lines across short distances, but commonly used by nineteenth-century gangs as a weapon.

36   Musket.

37   See Appendix 3 for examples of the coverage of the California House Riot.

38   See Appendix 3 for a longer extract from Taylor's "Message."

APPENDIX 1.
LIFE AND ADVENTURES OF CHARLES ANDERSON CHESTER

1   "Turn out" refers to carriage equipment, including the dressing of horses and the driver's outfit. "Brag" is a card game of British origins, popular with gamblers.

2   The Merchants' Exchange Building, a brokerage house, was bounded by Dock, Walnut, and Third Streets in Philadelphia.

3   Injunction.

4   Your.

5   Pockets.

6   Charles's.

7   Their.

8   Bloodgood's Hotel in Philadelphia was at Walnut Street and Delaware Avenue; there may have been a Bloodgood's in New York City as well.

9   Cuban.

10   Throughout, probably intended to be "supernumerary"; corrected in *The Killers*. Here, however, it might also be intended as a mocking imitation of a popular contemporary pronunciation.

11   Here and in several places to follow, probably intended to be "gentleman."

12   With.

13   At.

14   Followed.

15   Nabob. The term derives from the Anglo-Indian context and refers to a conspicuously wealthy man who has made his fortune through corrupt trade.

16   There.

17   Lippard's analogy here makes reference to conflicts in Texas between new Anglo settlers and Mexican ranchers, culminating in the Mexican-American War (1846–48), which followed the annexation of Texas by the United States.

18 Murmur.

19 Through.

20 The lowlands and marshy areas south of Philadelphia, between the converging Schuylkill and Delaware Rivers—popular combat grounds for intergang conflict, among other associations of this time—were known as "The Neck."

21 Livid.

22 Negro.

APPENDIX 2. INTRODUCTION TO
THE SERIALIZED VERSION OF *THE KILLERS*

1 Edward Coke (1552–1634) and William Blackstone (1723–80), famed English jurists whose writings on law were standard references.

2 One of Lippard's earliest journalistic assignments in Philadelphia was to cover the investigation of spending on the construction of Girard College, founded by Stephen Girard (1750–1831) as a boarding school exclusively for fatherless children. The school's foundation later became controversial for the mishandling of Girard's legacy, which languished for years in the bank of a prominent Philadelphian, Nicholas Biddle, who was brought to trial for fraud.

APPENDIX 3. RELATED CONTEMPORARY DOCUMENTS

1 The Hutchinson Family Singers were a popular singing group that toured widely in the 1840s and 1850s. As implied here, they sang and composed abolitionist songs and engaged other political issues of the time, including temperance, women's rights, and labor conflict.

2 Pennsylvania Hall in Philadelphia, built by the Pennsylvania Anti-Slavery Society, was burned by a mob on May 18, 1838, a few days after it had been opened.

3 The Astor Place riot, a riot fueled by class tensions and nativism, had happened earlier that year (May 10, 1849); dozens of people were killed or injured in it, and the state militia was called in by the mayor of New York City to quell it.

4 The 1818 act was one of several, following the 1807 banning of the importation of slaves and prior to emancipation, that contributed to the suppression of the slave trade, in part by pressuring slaveholders to maintain proof that slaves had been acquired domestically rather than internationally.

5 For "Chili," read Chile. These territories—one of them the final destination of the novella's characters Kate and Elijah—had seen exponential population growth and international attention in the wake of the gold rush that began in January of 1848. California would be admitted to the Union in 1850; Oregon, in 1859.

6 Taylor's "Message," dated December 4, 1849, was transmitted to Congress December 24, 1849.

INDEX

Index

Index

Index

racial mixing: and California House Riot, 15; and Moyamensing district, 16, 24, 200; and Runnel's Court, 24, 69

racial violence: in *Chester*, 198–201, 207–10; contributing factors, 20–21, 24–25; Philadelphia's history of, 16–18, 20–21, 24–25; in *The Killers*, 7–8, 121, 127–28, 144–45, 162

racism, and labor competition, 24–25

real estate practices: and Jacob Hicks, 91; and Respectable Killers, 214

Redburn: His First Voyage (Melville), 5

reformism, middle-class: as Lippard target, 5; and solitary confinement policy, 7, 9–10, 84–85, 115

religion, pursuit of money as, 64, 65, 91

religious hypocrisy: as Lippard theme, 4; in *The Killers*, 94–95, 97–98, 115; and Vestry Room Killers, 214

"Respectable Killers," 26, 40–41, 164, 214–16

Reynolds, David, on Lippard, 3, 6, 235–36n10

romans-feuilletons, 8

Rookwood (Ainsworth), 9

Runnel's Court: and Black Andy's groggery, 106; described, 69; as Elijah's home, 67; as liminal space, 24; as working-class home, 21, *22*, 24

Sara Jane (sailing vessel), 54, 78–80, 82–83, 135

Saratoga, 48, 53, 239n3

sensational journalism: and printing technologies, 4; publishing practices, 12

sentimentalism, literary, Lippard's attacks on, 5

serial sensation novel: emergence of, 8–9; and publishing practices, 12; *The Quaker City* as, 4

Seventh Ward, 16

Severns, Joseph, as Lippard's partner, 12, 14

Shadow and Light: An Autobiography (Gibbs), 24–25

Sixth and St. Mary Streets, 16, 21, 127–28, 131, 200–201, 204, 227

slave trade: and act of Congress (1818), 230, 242n4; as act of piracy, 38; and Cromwell, 37–38, 88, 124, 125; and Cuban annexation, 36–38; and Don Jorge, 37–38, 160; and Jacob Hicks, 38–39, 64, 92, 134; linked with class/wealth, 15, 38–39, 64, 92, 124,

158, 163; and Velasquez, 92, 134, 158; and Zachary Taylor's message to Congress, 230–32

Smith, Caleb, 10

solitary confinement: and Clifford Pyncheon (Hawthorne character), 10; as Eastern State Penitentiary policy, 7, 9–10, 84–85; *The Killers* as critique of, 9–11; vs. hanging, 84

Southwark district: foreign-born population, 16; map of, *172*; Monk Hall as embodiment, 21

speculation, and Jacob Hicks, 91–92

"The Spermaceti Papers" (Lippard), 3

Spirit of the Times (Philadelphia newspaper), 3

Stowe, Harriet Beecher, 1

street gangs. *See* urban gangs

Sue, Eugène, 8, 10–11

Taylor, Zachary, 38, 164, 229–33

Thompson, George, 26

Tobiason, Aaron, 28

tuberculosis, and Lippard, 3, 6

Twain, Mark, and Lippard's works, 5

Uncle Tom's Cabin (Stowe), as best-seller, 1

underworld, exposed in *Charles Anderson Chester*, 15

urban gangs: hose companies' association with, 15, 30–33, *31*; as mainstay of city mystery genre, 30. *See also* the Killers (*Chester* gang); the Killers (*Killers* gang); the Killers (Philadelphia gang)

Walnut Street, as Jacob Hicks residence, 56, 73, 88

Washington and His Generals; or, Legends of the Revolution (Lippard), 20

Watson, H.C., 31

Webb, Frank J., 11, 20

Whitman, Walt, and Lippard's works, 5, 11

Williams, James, 18

The Woman in White (Collins), 9

working class, as target readership of *The Killers*, 2

working-class consciousness: linked with blackness, 27–28; undermined by racism, 25

working-class issues, as Lippard priority, 4

working-class living conditions, epitomized by Runnel's Court, 21, *22*, 24

ACKNOWLEDGMENTS

The editors thank Caroline Winschel, Caroline Hayes, and Jerry Singerman at the University of Pennsylvania Press for their support of this project. We also thank Lara Langer Cohen and an anonymous reader for the press for suggestions that greatly strengthened the introduction. Jeannine DeLombard, Geoffrey O'Brien, Doug Armato, Christopher Looby, Robert Levine, David Reynolds, and Christopher Castiglia also offered encouragement and guidance. Thanks go to Helene Ferranti and to Sari Altschuler and Aaron Tobiason for sharing an early draft of their playbill discovery respecting Devil-Bug with us. Without the help of Jim Green, Phil Lapsansky, Connie King, Nicole Joniec, Hillary Kativa, and the rest of the staff at the Library Company of Philadelphia and the Historical Society of Pennsylvania, this book would not exist: thank you all.

Matt Cohen would like to thank Michael Winship, Ty Alyea, Caleb Smith, Lauren Grewe, and Christopher Labarthe for their help, in many and various ways, in making this book. Jace Everett, Daniel Weston Cohen, Michael Cohen, Kathy Cohen, and Marian Weston, these have a nifty knack: seeing nonsense, helping gloss my yammering, laying on valuable emendations, and always making things happier.

Edlie Wong would like to thank her family, Catherine Paiste, and her wonderful Philadelphia friends—Amze Emmons,

Acknowledgments

Adalaine Holton, James Ker, Jena Osman, Josephine Park, and James Salazar—for their support, good humor, and generosity as this book came into being.